The
Delaware Colony

by Dennis B. Fradin

Consultant: Barbara E. Benson
              Executive Director
              The Historical Society of Delaware

 CHILDRENS PRESS®
CHICAGO

Library of Congress Cataloging-in-Publication Data

Fradin, Dennis B.
  The Delaware Colony / by Dennis Brindell Fradin.
    p. cm. — (The Thirteen Colonies)
  Includes index.
  Summary: Discusses some of the key people and events in Delaware's
history, from the arrival of the first explorers in the 1600s to becoming the
first state in 1787.
  ISBN 0-516-00398-4
  1. Delaware—History—Colonial period, ca. 1600-1775—Juvenile literature.
2. Delaware—History—Revolution, 1775-1783—Juvenile literature.
[1. Delaware—History—Colonial period, ca. 1600-1775. 2. Delaware—History—
Revolution, 1775-1783. 3. Delaware—History—Confederation, 1783-1789.]
I. Title. II. Series: Fradin, Dennis B. Thirteen Colonies.
F167.F73   1992
975.1'02—dc20   92-10467
                                                                     CIP
                                                                      AC

     4 5 6 7 8 9 10 R 01 00 99 98 97

Table of Contents

Chapter I:
Introducing the First State...................................... 5

Chapter II:
The First People in Delaware 15

Chapter III:
Exploration and First Settlement............................... 25
Biographical sketch of Henry Hudson 39

Chapter IV:
The Period of Swedish Rule: 1638-1655 41
Biographical sketch of Peter Minuit 58
Biographical sketch of Johan Printz........................... 59

Chapter V:
The Period of Dutch Rule: 1655-1664.......................... 61

Chapter VI:
Early English Rule: 1664-1704 77
Biographical sketch of William Penn........................... 96

Chapter VII:
Years of Steady Growth: 1705-1760............................ 98

Chapter VIII:
Life in Colonial Delaware in the Early 1760s 109

Chapter IX:
The Revolutionary War Era: 1764-1783....................... 119
Biographical sketch of Caesar Rodney 138
Biographical sketch of Thomas McKean 139

Chapter X:
Delaware Becomes the First State!............................ 141
Biographical sketch of John Dickinson........................ 147

Documents:
Declaration of the Causes of Taking up Arms against England 150
Declaration of Independence 151

Colonial America Time Line 152

Index 155

Old Swedes Church (Trinity Church) in Dover, Delaware, is one of the oldest Protestant churches in the United States. Top left: The state seal of Delaware

---

Chapter I

Introducing the First State

A jewel among the States!

> *Thomas Jefferson, third President of the*
> *United States, describing Delaware*

Delaware is a very small state that lies along the Atlantic Coast of the eastern United States. It occupies part of the Delmarva Peninsula. A peninsula is land that is surrounded by water on three sides. Parts of Maryland and Virginia share the Delmarva Peninsula with Delaware. The name *Delmarva* comes from the words *Delaware, Maryland,* and *Virginia.*

Pennsylvania is Delaware's neighboring state to the north. Maryland lies to the west and to the south. To the east of Delaware are the waters of the Atlantic Ocean, Delaware Bay, and the Delaware River. The state of New Jersey lies to the east across the bay and the river.

If you turn a map of Delaware sideways so that the Atlantic Ocean, Delaware Bay, and the Delaware River are at the top, you will see that the

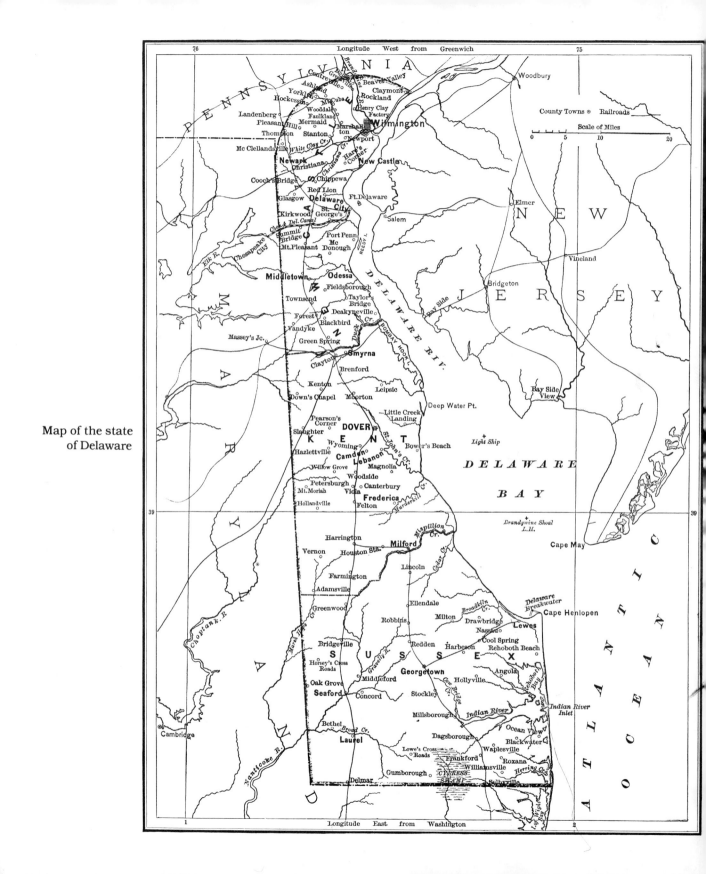

Map of the state
of Delaware

state is shaped like a shoe. Actually, on most maps of the United States, Delaware looks like an elf's shoe. Of all fifty states, only tiny Rhode Island is smaller than Delaware. Yet few states have as fascinating a history as Delaware.

For many centuries, a peaceful people called the Lenni-Lenape (later known as the Delaware) lived in the region. In 1638 the first European settlers in Delaware began arriving from Sweden. The Swedes made Delaware part of their only American colony, which was called *New Sweden*. Swedish colonists in Delaware built the first log cabins in America.

After only seventeen years, New Sweden was taken over by the Dutch (people from The Netherlands) in 1655. Delaware then became a part of the Dutch colony of New Netherland. Just as the Swedes introduced the log cabin, the Dutch brought many of their favorite things to America, ranging from Santa Claus to doughnuts.

New Netherland lasted only until 1664, when it was captured by the English. Delaware then became one of England's thirteen American colonies. In addition to Delaware, the colonies were Virginia, Massachusetts, New Hampshire, New York, Connecticut, Maryland, Rhode Island,

COLONIAL AMERICA

Pennsylvania, North Carolina, New Jersey, South Carolina, and Georgia.

Delaware was an English colony for more than a century. For most of that time, the region was controlled by the Penn family from nearby Pennsylvania. However, Delaware was left alone by the Penns and also by the mother country, England. When some Americans began to rebel against England in the early 1770s, most Delawareans were content to keep things as they were. Yet once the Revolutionary War (1775–1783) actually began, Delaware helped the United States break free of England. Several thousand Delawareans fought in George Washington's Continental Army, and in July 1776 Caesar Rodney made a famous ride to Philadelphia to make sure that Delaware declared its independence along with the other states.

Soon after the Revolutionary War was won, American leaders made a new set of national laws called the United States Constitution. Each of the thirteen former colonies would become a state under the new government the moment it approved the Constitution. Delaware approved the U.S. Constitution on December 7, 1787, before any of the other twelve states. This earned Delaware one of its nicknames, the *First State.*

Caesar Rodney

Delaware is also called the *Diamond State* because, like a diamond, it is small but valuable. And it is nicknamed the *Blue Hen State* because of a Revolutionary War battle cry discussed later in this book.

About eighty years after the Revolutionary War ended, Delaware played an important role in another war, the Civil War (1861–1865). This war was fought because the Southern states wanted the U.S. government to stay out of certain matters, such as whether or not a state could have slavery. Eleven Southern states withdrew from the Union and formed their own country, the Confederate States of America, which fought the Northern, or Union, states.

The Blue Hen chicken is the state bird of Delaware.

Delaware was a border state—situated between the North and the South. Which side would Delaware join? Although Delaware allowed slavery and was like the Southern states in other ways, it had been the first state to join the Union and had close ties to Pennsylvania, which stood firmly with the Union. In the end, a few hundred Delaware men fought for the Confederacy, but nearly 15,000 others fought for the Union.

Meanwhile, during the 1800s, the way people earned their living was changing in many states, including Delaware. In the 1700s, most of the

Workers at the DuPont plant in the nineteenth century

people were farmers. But in the early 1800s, manufacturing grew in importance and more people were making products rather than farming. A Frenchman named E. I. du Pont helped develop manufacturing in Delaware.

E. I. du Pont (1771–1834) arrived at Brandywine Creek near Wilmington, Delaware, in 1801. There he built a gunpowder factory which grew into the world's largest chemical firm, the famous DuPont Company. A number of other chemical companies also set up headquarters in Wilmington, which became known as the "Chemical Capital of the World." In addition, factories that made iron and steel products, leather goods, and cloth products were built in Wilmington and other Delaware cities during the 1800s. Today the raising of broiler chickens is the only major farming activity in which Delaware ranks near the top nationally. About fifteen Delawareans now work at manufacturing for each person who farms—the reverse of the situation in colonial days. Chemicals and packaged foods are Delaware's top products.

John Dickinson

Because of its size, Delaware has always had to scrape and scrounge to keep up with the larger states. In colonial days, its leaders had to scramble at times just to preserve Delaware's existence. In 1899, the state government passed a law making it easier for businesses to set up their corporate headquarters in Delaware than in other states. Over the years, this law has attracted many companies to the First State even though they do little or no business in the state.

Considering its size, Delaware has been home to a large number of famous people besides the patriot Caesar Rodney and the manufacturer E. I. du Pont. John Dickinson (1732–1808) was born in Maryland but lived much of his life in Delaware.

11

Annie Jump Cannon

Howard Pyle

Richard Allen

Thomas Garrett

Dickinson became known as the "Penman of the Revolution" because of the important papers he wrote when the United States was breaking free of England. Astronomer Annie Jump Cannon (1863–1941) was born in Dover, Delaware. She was nicknamed the "Census Taker of the Sky" because of all that she discovered about the stars.

Howard Pyle (1853–1911), who was born in Wilmington, became a famous author and illustrator of children's books, including *The Merry Adventures of Robin Hood*. Also born in Wilmington was author John Marquand (1893–1960), whose novel *The Late George Apley* won the 1937 Pulitzer Prize for literature.

Delaware has also produced several well-known people who worked to help African Americans. Richard Allen (1760–1831), a slave born in Pennsylvania, was sold to a Delaware plantation owner. Allen became a preacher while still a slave. After saving enough money to buy his freedom, he organized the African Methodist Episcopal Church, the first black church denomination in the United States. Thomas Garrett (1789–1871) was a white man who turned his Wilmington home into a stop on the "Underground Railroad," the system by which slaves escaped to freedom in the Northern states and Canada.

Cypress swamps are part of the diverse scenery of Delaware.

Besides having a fascinating history and many famous people, Delaware is also very lovely. Wilmington, its largest city, has only about 70,000 people, making it just one quarter the size of nearby Philadelphia. No other city in Delaware has as many as 30,000 people. Dover, the capital, has only about 25,000 people, making it one of the least populous of the fifty state capitals.

Delaware's countryside is dotted with small towns, coastal beaches, forests, and even swamps. The state has a surprising amount of wildlife, especially in such protected areas as Bombay Hook National Wildlife Refuge on Delaware Bay. Deer, beavers, foxes, muskrats, otters, turtles, and hundreds of kinds of birds can still be seen, though not in the large numbers that once lived there when Native Americans were Delaware's only people.

Settlers of New Sweden trading with the Native Americans

Chapter II

The First People in Delaware

*Regardless of his nationality or skin color, a visitor
[to a Lenni-Lenape village] would have been
greeted with warm hospitality. Deeply ingrained in
the Delawares' tradition was the obligation they felt
to share their food and the comfort of their wigwams
with a stranger.*

From The Delaware Indians: A History, *by C.
A. Weslager*

People have lived in Delaware for at least 1,500
years. Delaware's oldest known relics were found
accidentally by road builders in 1928. Consisting
of human and animal skeletons, shells, stone
tools, and clay bowls, these relics were uncovered
near Delaware Bay in the eastern part of the state.
However, since people lived in nearby Pennsylvania and New Jersey at least 10,000 years ago,
much older remains may someday be unearthed
in Delaware, too.

Long before the first colonists arrived, a people
who called themselves the Lenni-Lenape, meaning
"Original People," were the main tribe in the
Delaware region. (These Native Americans are

The Native Americans
made carvings on
stones. This rock
carving was found
near Dingman's Ferry
in Sussex County,
New Jersey.

Wigwams were made of a framework of poles covered with bark. Several families might live in a wigwam.

also known as the Delaware, the name given to them by English colonists of the 1600s.) Approximately 10,000 Lenni-Lenape inhabited America before the colonists arrived. They lived in the Delaware River region of present-day Delaware as well as in Pennsylvania, New Jersey, and New York.

The Lenni-Lenape lived in villages of fifty to two hundred people. Their homes, called wigwams, were round or oblong huts made of wood and bark. Several related families lived in a wigwam,

16

each with its own section. Every village had its own chiefs and other leaders and was independent of all other Lenni-Lenape villages.

Near the wigwams were the fields where corn, beans, and squash were grown. The women and children grew the crops, using hoes made of the shoulder bones of deer to till the land. The men and their older sons fished with nets and hooks and hunted deer, bears, and other animals with bows and arrows. The women and children often

Lenni-Lenape women were in charge of the farming. They raised corn, beans, and squash.

Lenni-Lenape men were responsible for hunting and fishing.

accompanied the hunters, leaving the elderly men and women in charge of the village.

The women and their daughters prepared the food. Corn was served many different ways, including "on the cob," in the form of corn bread, mixed with beans in what was called "succotash," and blended with meat and fish in stews. A beaver's tail cooked in bear grease was considered a great delicacy. A kind of candy made of cornmeal and maple sugar was a favorite dessert among the children.

Families tended to be small, which was one reason why the Native American population never grew very large. A Lenni-Lenape mother carried her baby on a cradle board fastened to her back. When she went to tend the crops, she hung the cradle board with the child in it on a tree branch. The mother could watch her baby as the breeze rocked the child to sleep.

Instead of going to school, Lenni-Lenape children learned by working alongside their parents and other elders. Girls learned to farm and cook by helping their mothers. Boys were taught to hunt and fish by their fathers. Grand-parents and great-grandparents were very important to the family, too. Besides watching the village when everyone else was off hunting, the older people made tools and clay bowls, knitted fishing nets, and made clothing from animal skins.

The older people also taught Lenni-Lenape values and beliefs to the children. Young people were taught to live peacefully if possible, and to treat other people (including strangers) kindly. They were also taught that they must always avenge serious wrongs done to their family.

If you were lost in the Delaware woods back in the 1500s, meeting a Lenni-Lenape would be the best thing that could happen to you. Once you showed that you meant no harm, you would be led to the village. The villagers would offer you the best food and the best wigwam, and you would be allowed to stay as long as you wanted. Anyone who was unkind to you would be disgraced, just as you would be considered disgraced if you didn't welcome one of them into your home.

But suppose you killed the person that you met in the woods. Then you would find out about Lenni-Lenape justice! The dead person's family would avenge the murder. Their first choice would be to kill you. If they couldn't find you, their second choice would be to kill a member of your family. If they couldn't do that either, their third choice would be to kill another person of your kind. Lenni-Lenape children were known to wait fifteen years—until they had grown up—to avenge the murder of relatives.

Although the Lenni-Lenape sought revenge and fought wars when necessary, they were generally one of North America's most peaceful tribes. In fact, other tribes asked the Lenni-Lenape to settle their disputes and called them "Grandfathers" out of respect. In return, the Lenni-Lenape called the other tribes "Our Grandchildren."

Like other Native Americans, the Lenni-Lenape were very religious. They felt that a multitude of spirits lived in the woods, rivers, and sky. Above the lesser spirits were eleven important gods and goddesses: the Three Grandfathers (gods of the North, East, and West); Our Grandmother (the goddess of the South); the Earth, Elder Brother Sun, Elder Brother Moon, the Corn Mother, Fire, Water, and Home. Above these eleven gods and goddesses was the twelfth and most important god of all, *Kee-shay-lum-moo-kawng*, meaning "Our Creator."

According to a story the older Lenni-Lenapes told the children, long ago the world was all ocean. The Creator raised a Giant Turtle from deep in the water. As the Giant Turtle emerged into the sunlight, a tree began to grow from its back. Two of the tree's branches turned into the first man and woman. The Lenni-Lenape believed that they were descended from these first two people, and that all of the Earth's land rested on the Giant Turtle's back.

According to the Lenni-Lenape story, the first man and woman came from the tree that grew on the back of Giant Turtle.

Many Native Americans had a number that was special to them. The Lenni-Lenape's special number was 12, perhaps because the Giant Turtle was said to have 12 plates in its shell. The 12 important gods and goddesses were thought to live in 12 heavens, with the Great Spirit inhabiting the highest heaven. The tribe's yearly religious festivals, which included the Corn Dance in honor of the Corn Mother, sometimes lasted 12 days.

The Lenni-Lenape felt that babies were close to the spirit world, which they had left at birth. Parents didn't name their babies for some time after birth for fear that ghosts might learn their names and lure them back to the spirit realm. The children were named only when the parents felt they were firmly rooted in this world. And Lenni-Lenape parents rarely spanked or yelled at their children. They thought that such actions would make the Creator think the children were unloved and take them back to the spirit realm.

We know a lot about the Lenni-Lenape because they were the main tribe in the Delaware-Pennsylvania-New Jersey region when the colonists arrived. The several thousand Lenni-Lenapes who live today in Oklahoma, Wisconsin, and Canada have also told us about their customs and beliefs. We know less about the Nanticokes and Assateagues, smaller tribes that lived in both southern Delaware and the eastern shore of Maryland. In general, however, the Nanticokes and the Assateagues had a way of life similar to that of the Lenni-Lenape.

A Nanticoke dancer performs at a powwow in Millsboro, Delaware. Today, there are about 500 Nanticoke.

Most of the Native Americans were pushed out of Delaware by the European colonists who started to arrive in the 1600s. Today, only about 1,500 Indians live in Delaware, and only a few are related to the Native Americans who lived there during the 1500s.

The English ship *Vanguard* attacking the Spanish Armada. Spain's
attempt to invade England in 1588 was defeated by the English navy.

Chapter III

Exploration and First Settlement

A white sandy shore and within it an abundance of green trees.

> *Delaware as viewed in 1609 by Henry Hudson, the first known European explorer in the region*

THREE POWERFUL NATIONS

Colonial Delaware had a complex history. In fact, it bounced back and forth like a Ping-Pong ball between three powerful European nations—England, The Netherlands, and Sweden.

England was the strongest of the three. In 1588, England won a great sea battle against a fleet from Spain called the Armada. This helped launch England's "Golden Age"—a period when that country increased its power and excelled in the arts and science. The famous playwright William Shakespeare was one of the people who lived in England during that time.

25

For many people, life was far from perfect in England during its "Golden Age." For one thing, many families lived in dreadful poverty. Because of an English law that left most of a father's wealth to the oldest son, many people from wealthy families had financial problems, too. The country also was getting crowded. In addition, there was widespread religious persecution in England. Many people who criticized or abandoned the nation's official religion—the Church of England—lost their jobs and were imprisoned.

One of the many poor families in England receives bread at a rich man's gate.

A village in The Netherlands protected by a dike.

By the early 1600s, thousands of English people wanted to find a place where they could worship freely, and thousands more wanted to live where they could obtain land and wealth.

The 1600s were also a "Golden Age" for The Netherlands, a small nation located about two hundred miles east of England across the North Sea. A large part of The Netherlands (which means "Lowlands") lies below sea level. The Dutch had actually "stolen" much of their country from the sea by building seawalls called dikes to hold back the water.

Perhaps no other nation has ever accomplished as much in one century as The Netherlands did in the 1600s. Both the microscope and the telescope were invented around the year 1600 in The

A woman of
The Netherlands

Gustavus Adolphus

Netherlands. The great Dutch painters Rembrandt, Frans Hals, and Jan Vermeer were at work during the 1600s, as was the famous philosopher Baruch Spinoza. The Netherlands also was a leader in exploration—its sea captains sailed the world from Asia to Australia to North America. But this small nation had a major drawback when it came to sending people to colonize distant lands. The country was so noted for its religious freedom and respect for basic human rights that few people wanted to leave!

Sweden was the third nation that played a role in the story of colonial Delaware. Today, Sweden is one of the world's most peaceful nations, but that was not the case in the 1600s. Between 1611 and 1632 Sweden was ruled by Gustavus Adolphus, a warrior king who fought and defeated Denmark, Poland, and Russia. Gustavus Adolphus added so much territory to Sweden that the country grew to twice the size it is today.

But, like the Dutch, few Swedes wanted to leave home. Sweden had only about a million people in the early 1600s, which left plenty of room for everyone. The Swedish people also enjoyed a great deal of personal freedom compared with some other European countries.

FIRST EXPLORATIONS OF DELAWARE

The first permanent European settlement in what is now the United States was St. Augustine, which the Spanish founded in their Florida Colony in the fall of 1565. St. Augustine is the oldest European-built city in the United States. Nearly forty-two years later, in the spring of 1607, the English built their first permanent settlement in what is now the United States—Jamestown, Virginia.

For a while it appeared that Jamestown wouldn't last very long. During the winter of 1609–10, about 450 of the colony's 500 people died of starvation or disease. In June 1610, the few survivors were about to abandon Jamestown when three ships filled with supplies arrived under the command of Lord De La Warr (Thomas West). The supplies brought by Lord De La Warr enabled the settlers to revive Jamestown and enlarge the Virginia Colony. Lord De La Warr served as Virginia's governor for about a year and did a great deal to help the young colony.

Although he may have viewed Delaware from a distance, Lord De la Warr never set foot there. But to remember him for his services to Virginia, his name (with a slight change in spelling) was given to several places north of Virginia and also to a

Lord De La Warr arrives at
Jamestown, Virginia.

group of people. Delaware Bay and the Delaware
River that flows into it were both named for Lord
De La Warr, and the English called the Lenni-
Lenape people the Delaware. Pennsylvania, New
York, and four other states also have a Delaware
County. And, of course, the colony that became
the state of Delaware was also named for Lord De
La Warr.

The first known European explorer in the
Delaware region arrived in 1609. He was Henry
Hudson, an Englishman working for The Nether-
lands. The Dutch wanted to trade with Asian

countries, which people called the East Indies back then. To reach the East Indies, they had to travel by land across Europe or sail around Africa's southern tip. Both routes were difficult and dangerous. A trading firm called the Dutch East India Company hired Hudson to search for a shortcut to the East Indies by sailing across the Arctic waters of the North Pole region! At that time, people believed that a ship could sail across the top of the world, to Asia.

With a small crew that included his son, John, Hudson sailed the *Half Moon* northeast from The

Henry Hudson

Henry Hudson's ship *Half Moon*

Netherlands in early spring of 1609. However, ice prevented the *Half Moon* from sailing through polar waters.

Also at that time, many people believed that an inland waterway cut across the present-day United States toward Asia. Just so his voyage wouldn't be a total loss, Hudson decided to sail west in search of this non-existent shortcut through America to Asia. The *Half Moon* reached the coast of Newfoundland, Canada, in the summer of 1609. Henry Hudson first skimmed down the East Coast between Newfoundland and North Carolina. Then he turned the *Half Moon* back northward to make a more thorough search for the inland waterway.

On August 28, 1609, during this closer study of the East Coast, Hudson reached Delaware. He sailed past Cape Henlopen in southeastern Delaware into Delaware Bay, and then went a short way up the Delaware River. Seeing that the Delaware River wound northward and wasn't the fabled western waterway across America, he left the region. However, Hudson was impressed by his distant view of Delaware, which in those days was almost all forestland. He said it looked like "a white sandy shore and within it an abundance of green trees."

Henry Hudson reached this point on the Delaware River before turning back to England.

Henry Hudson headed home in late 1609, disappointed that he had not found the western waterway to Asia. He had no idea that history would honor him as the European discoverer of two great rivers—the Hudson in present-day New York State and the Delaware. And he did not know that The Netherlands would claim a large chunk of American land, including Delaware, based on his voyage.

In August 1610—almost a year after Hudson's arrival—an English sea captain named Samuel Argall entered Delaware Bay quite by accident. Argall was trying to sail from Virginia to Bermuda

Dutch people of the 1600s

when a storm blew him off course. He sought
shelter in what is now called the Harbor of Refuge
behind Delaware's Cape Henlopen. It was Captain
Argall who named the bay after Lord De La Warr,
and the name later spread to the river, the Lenni-
Lenape, and the Delaware Colony.

The Dutch had their own place names. For
example, the rivers the English called the Hudson
and the Delaware were known as the North River
and the South River to the Dutch. However, we are
using the English names throughout this book.

THE DUTCH SETTLEMENT OF ZWAANENDAEL

Based on Henry Hudson's voyage, the Dutch
claimed parts of what are now New York, New
Jersey, Connecticut, and Delaware. They called

their American territory New Netherland, and later added part of Pennsylvania to it.

Small numbers of Dutch people moved from The Netherlands to New Netherland in the early 1600s. Some of them hoped to make a fresh start in a new country.

Others wanted to trade with the Native Americans. For a few tools and trinkets, the Dutchmen could buy beavers and other furs that could be made into fancy clothes.

The fur trade was a major source of wealth for the European settlers.

The seal of the
Dutch colony of
New Netherland
featured the beaver.

In the early 1620s the government of The Netherlands gave the Dutch West India Company, a trading firm, permission to trade and build settlements in New Netherland. The first settlement the company built in New Netherland was Fort Orange (now Albany), founded in 1624 in what is now New York State. The next year the Dutch founded New Amsterdam, which is now New York City. A few years later, in about 1630, the Dutch founded an outpost that is now part of Jersey City, New Jersey. In 1633 the Dutch built a small combination fort-trading post called the House of Hope where Hartford, Connecticut, now stands.

The first Dutch settlement in present-day Delaware was built on land purchased from the Lenni-Lenape at what is now the town of Lewes at the mouth of Delaware Bay. It was called *Zwaanendael*, which means "Valley of the Swans," and was intended mainly as a whaling, fishing, and fur-trading outpost. Twenty-eight men from The Netherlands reached Zwaanendael in the spring of 1631. They were joined by five other men from New Amsterdam.

In December 1632, a Dutch sailor named David Pieterssen de Vries arrived at Zwaanendael and was horrified by what he found. The settlement was burned and human bones lay scattered across the ground. A Native American told de Vries what had happened.

The Dutch had put up a piece of tin with The Netherlands' coat of arms on it. Native Americans (probably the Lenni-Lenape), who came and went freely at Zwaanendael, did not realize that the

David Pieterssen de Vries

De Vries found the ruins of Zwaanendael.

coat of arms was an important symbol to the Dutch. When someone took down the piece of tin (and, some sources say, made it into a tobacco pipe), the Dutch were outraged. Someone, either a Dutchman or another Indian, killed the man who took the coat of arms. The dead man's family were enraged that he had been killed over a piece of tin. Feeling that the Dutch were to blame, they killed the settlers in Zwaanendael. One man reportedly escaped, but it is not known what became of him.

Although it had lasted just a short time, Zwaanendael played a crucial role in Delaware history. In fact, as we will discuss later, Delaware might have become part of Maryland if not for Zwaanendael. Despite the Zwaanendael fight, over the next few years the Dutch and the Lenni-Lenape continued to trade in the Delaware region, but Europeans did not try to build any more settlements in Delaware for some time.

HENRY HUDSON (?–1611)

Henry Hudson was born in England, although we don't know where or when. Historians think that he must have worked as a sailor, but we don't know that for sure either. All we know about Hudson occurred during the last few years of his life when he made four famous voyages.

In 1607 an English trading firm called the Muscovy Company hired Henry Hudson to sail to Asia over the North Pole. That spring Hudson left England in the *Hopewell*, but the ship was blocked by ice in the Arctic Ocean far from the North Pole and had to return to England.

The following spring, the Muscovy Company sent Hudson out in the *Hopewell* a second time to search for a polar route to Asia. Hudson's second voyage was also stopped cold by ice.

After these two failures, the Muscovy Company decided not to send Henry Hudson out again. However, the Dutch East India Company still believed in an ice-free route to Asia through the Arctic Ocean. Since no one knew Arctic waters better than Henry Hudson, the Dutch hired him to sail the *Half Moon* northeast across the Arctic Ocean to Asia.

Hudson left on this, his third and most famous expedition, in early spring of 1609. Once again, he found the polar route to Asia blocked by ice, so he sailed the *Half Moon* south to Delaware and other places in what is now the United States. Not only was Henry Hudson disappointed at not finding a waterway through America, he also found himself in trouble when he landed in England in late 1609. The Dutch were annoyed with him for sailing to America without permission, and the English were angry that he had sailed under The Netherlands' flag, rather than England's. English merchants then decided to send Henry Hudson on a fourth voyage to see if he could find a passage to Asia.

Henry Hudson sailed the *Discovery* out of England in April 1610. With him were his son, John, who had been with him on the three previous expeditions, and about twenty other men. Once in Canada, Hudson and his crew explored the bodies of water that were later named the Hudson Strait and Hudson Bay after him. Late in the year, the *Discovery* was frozen in by ice in the Hudson Bay. Hudson and his crew spent the winter of 1610–11 aboard the *Discovery* and in a little shelter they built on shore. The men suffered severely from cold and disease.

Several of Hudson's crew blamed him for getting them into this situation. They also thought that when the ice broke up, Hudson might want to continue searching for the westward passage to Asia rather than return home. In June 1611, Hudson's enemies seized him, his son John, and a few other men. They set them adrift in a tiny boat without food or water and then sailed the *Discovery* back toward England.

We don't know what happened to the Hudsons and their companions. They probably died shortly after being set adrift. As for the mutineers, several were killed in a fight with Eskimos. The others reached England where they were tried for mutiny, but were found not guilty.

In 1638, the first Swedish settlers arrived to begin the
New Sweden Colony.

Chapter IV

The Period of Swedish Rule: 1638–1655

The soil is by nature suitable for all kinds of agriculture and the cultivation of all kinds of rare fruit-bearing trees. Yet [it is] such a fertile country that the pen is too weak to describe, praise, and extol it. On account of its fertility it may well be called a land flowing with milk and honey.

> *Description of the Delaware region by Peter Lindeström, who came to New Sweden in 1654*

While the Dutch were gradually expanding New Netherland in places outside present-day Delaware, Sweden was thinking of starting an American colony. Sweden's great warrior king, Gustavus Adolphus, had died in 1632, the year David Pieterssen de Vries found Zwaanendael destroyed. The king's daughter, Christina, then became queen. Since Queen Christina was only six years old, her chancellor, Axel Oxenstierna, ruled Sweden. Oxenstierna and the young queen carried out her father's plans to support the colonization of America.

Late in 1637, Sweden sent two ships carrying several dozen men to begin its New Sweden Colony. One ship was named *Kalmar Nyckel (Key of Kalmar)*, after a fortress that guarded the city of Kalmar, Sweden. The other was the *Vogel Grip (Bird Griffin)*, after a legendary creature that was part-eagle and part-lion.

Peter Minuit

At this time the Dutch and Swedes were rivals but not bitter enemies. In fact, some people who wanted to colonize America worked part of the time for The Netherlands and part of the time for Sweden. Peter Minuit, the leader of this first Swedish expedition to America, had once served as governor of New Netherland. In that capacity, Minuit had made the most famous land purchase in United States history. In 1626, he bought Manhattan Island (now part of New York City) from some Native Americans for cloth and other trade goods worth about $24. However, officials in The Netherlands had accused Minuit of granting too much land to some wealthy men, and in 1631 he had been removed as governor of New Netherland. Six years later, Minuit was hired by the Swedes to lead their first expedition to America. A handful of Swedish and Dutch soldiers sailed across the Atlantic Ocean to build a fort near the Delaware River.

Governor Minuit purchasing Manhattan Island from some
Native Americans

After a difficult journey, the *Kalmar Nyckel* and
the *Vogel Grip* reached Delaware Bay around April
1, 1638. The ships headed up the bay and then
continued up the Delaware River. Near what is
now the northeastern corner of Delaware, the two
ships veered westward two miles up a little
waterway that Minuit named the Christina River,
after Sweden's girl queen. Sometime around April

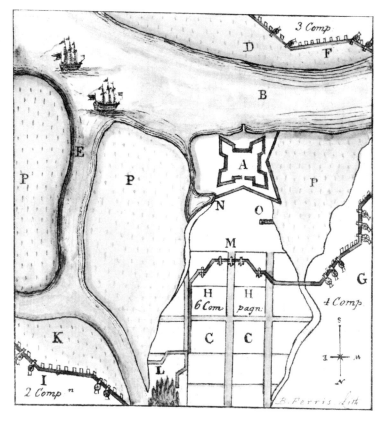

Early map of the town of Christina. Fort Christina, labeled A, is near the top.

8, 1638, Minuit anchored his ships at The Rocks, a natural wharf at present-day Wilmington.

Minuit soon purchased land from some Native Americans, much as he had bought Manhattan Island twelve years earlier for the Dutch. Minuit and his men built an outpost called Fort Christina at what is now Wilmington—the first permanent European settlement in Delaware. Fort Christina was also the first permanent settlement in New Sweden, which eventually extended along the Delaware River through what are now parts of Delaware, New Jersey, and Pennsylvania.

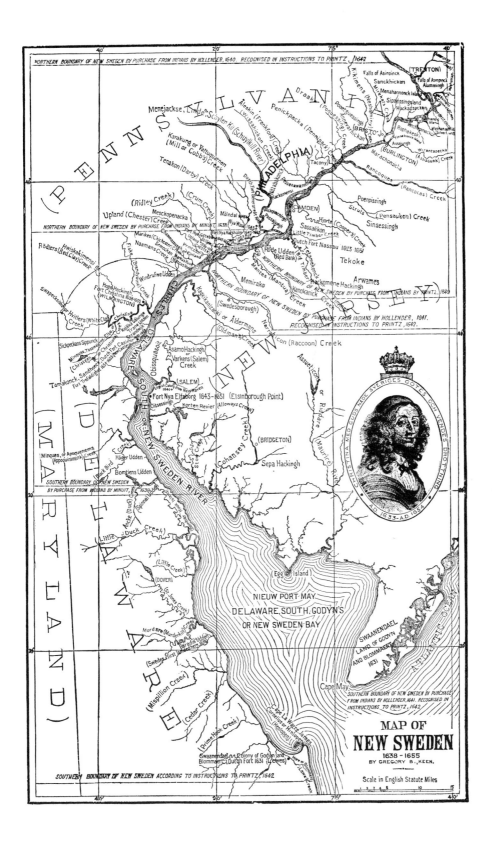

MAP OF
NEW SWEDEN
1638-1655
BY GREGORY B., KEEN.

Scale in English Statute Miles

Unfortunately, Peter Minuit died at sea while on a trading expedition the same year that he founded Fort Christina. Soon other ships arrived, bringing families, not just soldiers. However, very few Swedish families wanted to move to America.

Swedish soldier of the 1600s

Swedish officials thought of a way to obtain more colonists. They sentenced some Swedish army deserters and petty criminals to move to New Sweden! There were also many people who had crossed the border from Finland and broke Swedish conservation laws by burning forests to clear farmland and killing many wild animals just for their furs. Swedish officials rounded up some of these Finnish lawbreakers and sentenced them to move to New Sweden also. Few of the people who were sentenced to live in New Sweden were violent criminals. Upon reaching America, nearly all of them built farms and lived peaceful lives.

Even with the colonists who were forced to settle there, New Sweden never grew very large. In its seventeen years of existence, New Sweden's population never exceeded 1,000. These colonists lived in scattered little settlements along the Delaware River in Delaware, New Jersey, and Pennsylvania.

During the 1630s the Swedes and the Finns in Delaware built the first log cabins in America.

Settlers build a log cabin in the wilderness.

First they chopped down trees and cut them into logs. Then they cut notches into the corners of the logs, which they fitted together to make the cabins. Later, many thousands of American settlers besides the Swedes and the Finns built log cabins as they moved westward across the country.

Delaware's early log cabins had only one room. The windows were openings covered by sliding boards. Since they had no beds, the people slept on straw or leaves that they piled on the dirt floor. Fires for cooking and heating were built on the dirt floor, too. There were no chimneys at first, so the cabins were very smoky, although some of the smoke escaped through a hole in the roof. Nearly every family made their own tables and stools and even their plates, bowls, cups, and spoons out of wood.

The colonists had brought pigs, sheep, and cattle across the ocean with them, but they also hunted deer and other animals in the new country. Besides meat, the animals provided skins and wool for clothing. Corn, peas, beans, and turnips were the colonists' main crops. They also grew a great deal of tobacco, which they sold to Sweden. In fact, the colonists spent so much of their time and energy growing tobacco that they sometimes suffered from food shortages. When that happened, they traded for food with the Native Americans, the New Netherlanders, and the people of the English colonies.

In addition to the log cabin, the Finns and the Swedes also introduced the sauna to America. The sauna was a log sweathouse where the temperature was raised by means of a fireplace and heated rocks. A family would spend up to an hour in their sauna, then run outside and dive into the snow in cold weather or the river when it was warmer. This cleaned the body and really woke a person up, especially on winter mornings! More than 300 years later, many people still enjoy saunas.

"BIG BELLY" PRINTZ RULES NEW SWEDEN

New Sweden's first governor, Peter Minuit, had died at sea. The colony's second governor, Peter Hollandaer, was from The Netherlands like Minuit, but proved to be the wrong man for the job. Aside from buying some land, Hollandaer did little during his term (1640–43) to help New Sweden grow. In fact, his dislike of Swedes apparently inflamed other people's prejudices, too. During his term the Swedes argued a great deal with the Dutch people who had come to New Sweden. There also were shortages of food and supplies under Governor Hollandaer, as trade with other colonies dwindled.

In their early years, European colonies in America generally needed strong leaders to help them survive. The home countries knew this, and sometimes chose colonial governors who were so strong that they acted like tyrants. A case in point was Peter Stuyvesant, who governed New Netherland between 1647 and 1664. Stuyvesant was an old soldier who had lost a leg while serving as governor of some Dutch Islands in the Caribbean Sea. During his seventeen years as New Netherland's governor, Stuyvesant did a great deal to build up New Amsterdam (now New York City),

Peter Stuyvesant was the governor of New Netherland from 1647 to 1664.

but people complained that he bossed them around like the czar of Russia. Once when New Netherlanders threatened to tell the home country about his unfairness, "Stubborn Pete" said he would make anyone who complained "a foot shorter and send the pieces to [The Netherlands], and let him appeal in that way!"

Peter Hollandaer's replacement as New Sweden's governor was a man in the Stuyvesant mold. His name was Johan Printz, and he was the first governor of New Sweden who had been born in Sweden. Like Peter Stuyvesant, Printz had been a soldier; and, like the one-legged Stuyvesant,

Printz had a handicap: he weighed over 400 pounds. Upon seeing Printz, the Native Americans nicknamed him "Big Belly" and "the Big Tub."

Printz arrived at Delaware's Fort Christina in early 1643. His two ships carried several dozen new colonists and soldiers, and such vital supplies as peas, grain, clothes, guns, and horses. Despite the fact that only small numbers of people settled in New Sweden during his ten and a half years as governor, "Big Belly" Printz improved the colony through the sheer force of his personality.

Johan Printz

Governor Printz had his workers build several new forts and trading posts along the Delaware River, including Fort Elfsborg in New Jersey and New Gothenburg in Pennsylvania. New Gothenburg (named for a city in Sweden and located near what is now Philadelphia) was the first permanent European settlement in present-day Pennsylvania. Printz moved New Sweden's capital from Fort Christina to New Gothenburg, where he built not only a fort but also houses, a school, a church, and a mansion for his family. Called *Printzhof* (Printz Hall), this mansion was two stories tall and had brick fireplaces and glass windows.

Printz also worked to better farming and trade

in New Sweden. Under his supervision, New Sweden's settlers traded with the Native Americans for beaver skins and other furs, and shipped furs and tobacco back to Sweden. Realizing that New Sweden would fail without more help from the parent country, Printz wrote many letters home begging for more settlers and supplies. However, Sweden wasn't interested in helping its American territory succeed. By 1647, when New Sweden was nine years old and should have been growing rapidly, it had only several hundred people living on a small number of farms and forts along the Delaware River.

Meanwhile, The Netherlands, which still claimed the territory based on Henry Hudson's explorations, wanted to seize New Sweden. The Dutch Governor Peter Stuyvesant knew that New Sweden's small population was poorly defended. In the summer of 1651 Stuyvesant led an 11-ship fleet to the Delaware River. He had his men build Fort Casimir (at present-day New Castle, Delaware) about seven miles down the Delaware River from the Swedish Fort Christina. Governor Printz fumed, but, as Peter Stuyvesant had expected, he couldn't do anything about it.

The founding of Fort Casimir was the beginning of the end for New Sweden. Any ship wanting to

The town of New Amstel

sail up the Delaware had to pass Fort Casimir, so the Dutch now had control over river traffic. Governor Printz sent a protest to Stuyvesant, but since "Stubborn Pete" was a lot like himself, it did no good.

"Big Belly" Printz was also having trouble with his own settlers. They complained that he was brutal, made them work like slaves at Printzhof, and traded with the Native Americans for his own gain rather than the colony's. In 1653, twenty-two New Sweden colonists signed a petition complaining about Governor Printz. The Swedish governor then did what Peter Stuyvesant in New Netherland only threatened to do to protesters. He arrested the alleged ringleader, Anders Jönsson, tried him for treason (acting against the government), and hanged him. Printz then proclaimed himself innocent of the charges in the petition. After what he had done to Anders Jönsson, who would argue with Governor Printz?

By now, though, Printz wanted to return to Sweden with his family. He had never meant to stay so long in America, and he was also worried that his settlers might try to murder him. In the fall of 1653 Printz turned the governorship of New Sweden over to his son-in-law, Johan Papegoja, and prepared to sail to Sweden. Since no Swedish ships were available, Printz and his family had to travel to New Amsterdam and take a Dutch ship home. Although New Netherland and New Sweden were jockeying for control of New Sweden, they were still friendly enough that the Swedish governor could sail on a Dutch ship.

When he left America Governor Printz didn't know that Swedish officials were finally trying to help New Sweden. Two ships—the *Örn (Eagle)* and the *Gyllene Haj (Golden Shark)* had been chosen to carry about 350 colonists and soldiers as well as supplies to New Sweden. This expedition, which New Sweden so desperately needed, was supposed to leave for America around the time that former Governor Printz departed.

Because the *Gyllene Haj* leaked, its cargo and many of its passengers were squeezed into the *Örn*, which finally left Sweden in February 1654. The *Örn* encountered storms during the ocean crossing, and there were battles with enemy ships. Peter Lindeström, a member of the expedition who later wrote a book about New Sweden, reported that the *Örn*'s passengers had to eat rotten food "such as entirely decayed fish," and drink "putrid water." By the time the *Örn* reached Delaware Bay on May 18, 1654, disease had killed about 100 of its 350 passengers.

Johan Rising, the commander of the *Örn*'s expedition, had come to assist Governor Printz in New Sweden. Since Printz had already left, Johan Rising automatically replaced Printz's son-in-law, Johan Papegoja, as governor.

Soon after the *Örn* reached the Delaware River, Rising anchored the ship near the Dutch Fort Casimir. Governor Rising fired a salute from the *Örn* to the few Dutch soldiers in the little fort—the customary salute from a passing ship. However, the Dutch did not fire the customary return salute—and Governor Rising knew why.

Governor Johan Rising demanded that the Dutch surrender Fort Casimir.

The Dutch soldiers inside Fort Casimir did not have enough powder to fire a cannon!

Governor Rising decided to send some soldiers into the fort with a message ordering the Dutch to surrender. He fired a few shots from his ship's heavy guns to let the Dutch know he could back up his words. The Dutch defenders of Fort Casimir laid down their weapons. Down came the

Dutch flag and up went the Swedish flag. Since it was Trinity Sunday (a Christian holiday that comes about two months after Easter) of 1654, Governor Rising renamed the fort *Trefaldighet*, meaning "Trinity."

About twenty Dutch families lived on scattered farms around the fort. Several Dutchmen who were considered enemies of Sweden were forced to leave, but the others were told they could continue life as usual if they swore loyalty to Sweden. Not very concerned about which flag flew over their settlement, the Dutch people around Fort Trinity took the oath that made them citizens of New Sweden.

Peter Stuyvesant and other Dutch leaders were enraged when they learned about Rising's takeover of Fort Casimir, and soon took revenge by conquering New Sweden. Because of the consequences of his actions, Johan Rising has often been blamed for the downfall of Sweden's first and last American colony. But the real reason New Sweden came to an end was that Swedish officials had not built it into the kind of colony that could last.

PETER MINUIT (1580-1638)

Peter Minuit

One of the few known facts about Peter Minuit's early life was that he was born in the town of Wesel in what is now Germany, just twenty-five miles from The Netherlands. His ancestors are thought to have been Dutch, but they may have been French. *Minuit* means "midnight" in French, and Peter Minuit had a picture of a bat—a symbol of midnight—on his coat of arms. Minuit moved to The Netherlands, perhaps around 1624 when Spaniards captured his hometown of Wesel. He went to work for the Dutch West India Company, and did so well for them that by 1626 he was in America as the governor of New Netherland.

Minuit did a great deal to build New Netherland, especially the town of New Amsterdam where he had his headquarters. He supervised the construction of streets, homes, public buildings, and *bouweries* (Dutch for "farms") in New Amsterdam. To make sure that the Native Americans wouldn't claim Manhattan Island, which was the site of New Amsterdam, Governor Minuit bought it from some Indians for cloth, knives, and trinkets worth about $24. Minuit also established peaceful relations with the English Pilgrims who had founded the Plymouth Colony in Massachusetts.

Despite all that Minuit had done for New Netherland, Dutch officials felt that he had granted too much land to a few wealthy farmers. He was removed as New Netherland's governor in 1631 and soon returned to Europe. Feeling bitter toward the Dutch, Minuit then accepted an offer from their rivals, the Swedes, to help found New Sweden. Shortly after arriving in what is now the Wilmington region in the spring of 1638, he built Fort Christina, which was the start of New Sweden and Delaware's first permanent European settlement.

Peter Minuit kept peace with the Native Americans and with the people of other European colonies. Shortly after Fort Christina was built in the spring of 1638, Peter Minuit sailed down to the islands in the Caribbean Sea on a trading expedition, where he died in a hurricane. Perhaps New Sweden would have been more successful had Minuit lived.

JOHAN PRINTZ (1592–1663)

Johan Printz

Johan Printz had a peaceful background for someone who later became such a strong—and sometimes cruel—colonial governor. Born in Bottnyard, Sweden, Printz studied religion at universities in Germany with the intention of becoming a minister like his father. By the time Printz was twenty-seven years old, his father was dead and he was giving sermons in his father's old church at Bottnyard.

Apparently, Johan Printz was never ordained as a minister. While on a visit to Germany in 1620 he was kidnapped by a band of soldiers, and soon discovered that he preferred the military life to the ministry. For the next few years he hired himself out as a soldier to leaders in Austria, Germany, and Denmark. In 1625 Printz joined the Swedish army. He steadily rose in rank, and in 1639 he was placed in command of a Swedish force in Germany. There something happened that hurt his reputation.

In 1640, after Printz and his troops were defeated by a stronger German force, Printz left Germany without permission and returned home to Stockholm, Sweden. He was court-martialed for his actions. The court ruled that the defeat was not Printz's fault, but that he should not have abandoned his post. There is no record of his being punished. (Perhaps his appointment in 1642 as governor of New Sweden was a kind of punishment! Most Swedish military men of the time would have preferred a European post.)

Starting with the February day in 1643 that he arrived at Fort Christina, Johan Printz ruled New Sweden for ten and a half years. "Big Belly" was a terrible person in some ways. He executed a man just for leading a petition drive against him. He was often more concerned with his own gains than with his colony's welfare. Yet Printz must be credited with keeping New Sweden alive with little help from the parent country.

After more than a decade in America, Johan Printz left for Sweden in 1653 and never returned. He spent the last few years of his life as governor of his home district in Sweden, and died near his birthplace at the age of seventy after a fall from his horse.

View of New Amsterdam

Chapter V

The Period of Dutch Rule: 1655-1664

The Dutch settlers were not farmers, neither at New Amsterdam [now New York City] nor at New Amstel [now New Castle, Delaware]. They were town-dwellers, traders, and tradesmen. Their house [colony] had no foundations.

From The Dutch and Swedes on the Delaware: 1609-64 *by Christopher Ward*

THE FALL OF NEW SWEDEN

Once it was repaired, the *Gyllene Haj* followed the *Örn* to America. The people of New Sweden looked forward to the *Gyllene Haj*'s arrival with more colonists and supplies. The *Gyllene Haj* reached America in September 1654, several months after Johan Rising's capture of Fort Casimir, but there was one problem. Somehow the captain missed Delaware Bay by more than two hundred miles! Instead, he sailed the ship into New York Bay and up the Hudson River right into the hands of Governor Peter Stuyvesant at New Amsterdam.

Governor Stuyvesant seized the *Gyllene Haj* and its cargo. Stuyvesant treated the Swedish settlers aboard the vessel very kindly, however. In fact, he invited them to stay and become citizens of New Netherland.

Stuyvesant's offer appealed to the *Gyllene Haj*'s passengers. With 5,000 people, New Netherland had more than ten times New Sweden's population, and offered many more opportunities. Its capital, New Amsterdam, had shops, taverns, and schools and was well on its way to becoming a city. The town already had some Swedish people living there. One visitor to the town during the 1640s reported that eighteen different languages were spoken in New Amsterdam. Most of the *Gyllene Haj*'s passengers accepted Governor Stuyvesant's offer, depriving New Sweden of dozens of settlers.

As for Fort Casimir, Stuyvesant could have easily sent forces to win it back right away, but he awaited orders from The Netherlands. He knew that in the worldwide picture, New Netherland and New Sweden didn't mean very much to their home countries. Both nations valued their lands in other parts of the world more than they valued their American territories. If Stuyvesant plunged The Netherlands into a fight with Sweden over something as unimportant as New Sweden, he would be ruined. But if the home country told him to act against New Sweden, that would be a different story.

In late 1654 Stuyvesant received letters ordering him to not only win back Fort Casimir, but also to "drive the Swedes at the same time from the river [the Delaware]." Since all of New Sweden lay along the Delaware River, this meant that Stuyvesant was to conquer all of Sweden's American territory.

A few months later, in the summer of 1655, Stuyvesant organized a seven-ship fleet and more than 300 troops. He sailed this force down from New Netherland into Delaware Bay. On August 31, Stuyvesant and his men approached Fort Trefaldighet, which was still Fort Casimir to the Dutch.

This encounter could have resulted in a bloody battle. Sven Skute, the commander of the 75-man Swedish force at the fort, was under orders to stop any non-Swedish ship that came up the river without permission. A few hotheads, including Peter Lindeström, wanted to fight the Dutch forces, which would have been suicide. While meeting with a Dutch soldier who brought a demand to surrender, Lindeström said that the Swedes would fight "to the last man, or as long as there is a warm drop of blood in us."

However, most of the Swedish soldiers in the fort did not want to shed even one drop of blood over this hopeless cause. Some of them even climbed over the walls of the fort and joined Stuyvesant's forces. One deserter was climbing over the wall when he was shot in the leg by a fellow Swedish soldier. He proved to be the only casualty in the brief war between the Dutch and the Swedes over control of New Sweden.

Fortunately, Sven Skute had better judgment than the few hotheads who wanted to fight. During a meeting with Peter Stuyvesant, Skute realized that surrender was really his only choice. The surrender of the fort took place on September 1, 1655. Down came Sweden's yellow and blue flag from Fort Trefaldighet. Up went The Netherland's red, white, and blue flag over the same building, which was once again Fort Casimir!

Next, Stuyvesant took his forces north to Fort Christina, which was New Sweden's capital under Governor Johan Rising. To avoid bloodshed, Stuyvesant decided to lay siege to Fort Christina instead of attacking it. (A siege involves surrounding one's enemies and waiting until they give up because of a lack of food and supplies.)

To display Dutch power, Stuyvesant had his men fire some volleys from their big guns in the

Fort Casimir

direction of Fort Christina. Meanwhile, Dutch
soldiers attacked Swedish farmlands near the
fort, killing livestock and wrecking homes.

Governor Rising tried to hold out. He even sent
a message warning that Sweden might declare
war on The Netherlands if Stuyvesant didn't go
home to New Netherland. The Dutch and Swedes
should be friends, Rising also said, because they
were similar in many ways. He added that America
was big enough for both the Swedes and the

Dutch. But "Stubborn Pete" would not budge. His orders were to make New Sweden part of New Netherland.

Finally, after Fort Christina had been besieged for almost two weeks, Rising let his men vote on whether or not to surrender. The vote was unanimous—everyone chose to surrender! The terms that were worked out were not bad for New Sweden. True, the colony would be swallowed up by New Netherland and pass out of existence, but life wouldn't change much for its people. Families who wanted to return to Sweden would be transported there free of charge. Those who wanted to remain in their homes could do so. There was also a secret part of the treaty, and this is where Johan Rising seems to have acted selfishly and even dishonestly. He was to be paid a large sum of money for giving up New Sweden.

Before the treaty was signed, Governor Stuyvesant received bad news from New Amsterdam. While he had been off conquering New Sweden during the fall of 1655, an Indian girl had entered an orchard near what is now the corner of Broadway and Wall Street in New York City. The orchard's owner shot the girl dead for picking a few peaches. In revenge, the Indians attacked. They killed about one hundred Dutch settlers, took about one hundred and fifty prisoners, and badly damaged New Amsterdam and two settlements in New Jersey.

Compared to the "Peach War" back home, the New Sweden takeover suddenly seemed unimportant to Stuyvesant. The Dutch governor then made a surprising offer to the Swedes. He offered to return things to the way they had been before Rising's capture of Fort Casimir. The Dutch would keep Fort Casimir, but the Swedes would remain in charge of Fort Christina and the rest of New Sweden. All that had happened between the Swedes and the Dutch would be forgiven by both sides. Stuyvesant probably made this offer because he wanted to rush home and couldn't spare the troops needed to guard New Sweden.

These terms were almost exactly what Johan Rising had requested a few days earlier when he had sent the message to Stuyvesant. But Rising's response to Stuyvesant's offer was surprising. He refused it, and instead chose to give up all of New Sweden! Why?

In his written report, Rising said that with so many cattle killed and farms destroyed, New Sweden could not continue. Also, accepting Stuyvesant's offer would mean that Sweden couldn't sue The Netherlands for the damage to

New Sweden. In addition, Rising felt that accepting Stuyvesant's charity would have been a disgrace. We can add a fourth reason in Rising's behalf. After settling the problem in New Amsterdam, Stuyvesant might have returned and recaptured New Sweden. Some historians take a dim view of Rising's motives, though. They suggest that Rising didn't want to give up the money he had been offered for surrendering New Sweden.

Whatever Rising's motives were, the important fact was that when he and Peter Stuyvesant signed the treaty on September 15, 1655, New Sweden was dead. It was now part of New Netherland. This was the end of Sweden's attempts to colonize America.

DELAWARE UNDER DUTCH RULE

During his remaining month in America, Johan Rising went around telling his people to accept the free trip home to Sweden. Only a handful of people left with him, however. The rest felt that America was now their home, and they didn't care which flag they lived under as long as they were left in peace. They pledged their loyalty to The Netherlands and returned to their farms.

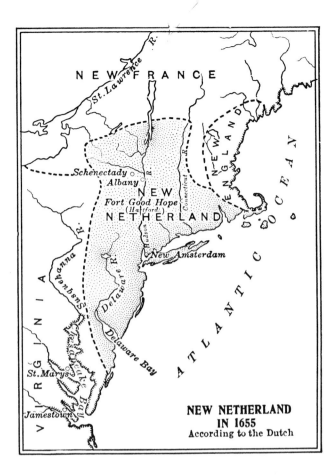

NEW NETHERLAND
IN 1655
According to the Dutch

There were a few changes in place names. Dutch officials weren't happy about Christina as the name for the fort and settlement at present-day Wilmington, so they changed the name to Altena. Fort Casimir and the little village that had grown up around it became New Amstel, after a river and town in The Netherlands.

The Dutch made New Amstel the capital of the Delaware region. Since the land around New Amstel was marshy, they did what they had done in The Netherlands. They drained the marshes and kept the water out by building dikes around the settlement. Then the Dutch built a two-story town hall and dozens of new homes. Hundreds of colonists, many of them Finnish people, moved to New Amstel. The settlement that had been home to about twelve families in 1655 had about one hundred buildings by the end of 1657. In fact, about as many people lived in New Amstel by then as had lived in all of New Sweden a few years earlier!

Also in 1657 the Delaware region was divided into two separate Dutch colonies—the City Colony and the Company Colony. The Christina River was the dividing line. The City Colony centered around New Amstel and owned the land south of the river to Bombay Hook. The colony was run by a governor appointed by the city of Amsterdam in The Netherlands. The Company Colony centered around Altena (now Wilmington) a short way to the north. It was run by the Dutch West India Company, which ran the rest of New Netherland and employed Peter Stuyvesant. Governor Stuyvesant appointed a deputy to rule this part of New Netherland for him. The City Colony and the Company Colony had a complex relationship. Not only is it difficult to understand today, it wasn't well understood by most people even during the 1650s!

One thing the colonists did know was that they wanted more self-government. In all the colonies—whether English, Swedish, or Dutch—the people were always clamoring for more say in their government. They had built their farms and towns and had sometimes fought Native Americans with little help from their mother countries. After doing all this, they resented taking orders from lawmakers 3,000 miles away across the Atlantic Ocean.

In New Amsterdam, the people had continually pestered Governor Stuyvesant for more self-rule. "Stubborn Pete" had finally allowed this in 1653. Starting that year, New Amsterdammers were allowed to have a *schout* (sheriff), five *schepens* (aldermen), and two *burgomasters* (mayors). At first Stuyvesant appointed these officials, but soon New Amsterdammers won the right to help choose them.

The people of New Amstel also wanted more of a voice in government. They achieved this in the late 1650s, not long after New Amsterdammers won the same right. The men of New Amstel were allowed to help select a number of their own officials, including three *burgomasters*, several *schepens*, a *schout*, and a council known as a *vroedschap*.

During the nine years (1655–1664) that Delaware was a Dutch territory, its population never became even half Dutch. Together, the Swedes and the Finns outnumbered the Dutch in Delaware. Yet the Dutch made many contributions to the colony's way of life.

The Dutch leaned more toward shopkeeping than did the Swedes or the Finns. In New Amsterdam they ran taverns, butcher shops, bakeries, tobacco shops, hotels, and dry goods stores. New

A Dutch household in New Amsterdam

Amstel was not large enough for the shoemakers, weavers, and tailors who came there hoping to set up a business. But the Dutch at New Amstel did manage to open a bakehouse, a yard for making bricks, and a forge for working with metals.

Unfortunately, the Dutch shopkeepers who came to Delaware weren't used to the farmwork that was necessary for survival, and some of them went hungry at first. When they had enough food, the Dutch ate a number of tasty dishes that they had introduced to America in New Amsterdam. For example, they made a cabbage salad in vinegar called *koosla* ("cole slaw"). The Dutch also introduced *olykoecks* ("doughnuts") and twisted cakes called *crullers* (meaning "to curl") to America. The Dutch had cakes for every occasion. After funerals they ate *doed-koecks* (dead-cakes), and on their *Sinterklaas* (Santa Claus) Day holiday they ate *speculaas* (spicy cakes).

Dutch families were probably the first people to introduce the Sinterklaas tradition into Delaware, as they had in New Amsterdam. Sinterklaas (called Saint Nicholas by the English) was said to leave gifts for good children on the night of December 5. The Sinterklaas customs slowly spread to the English colonies, but English children said *Sinterklaas* so quickly that the name became *Santa Claus*. The English also moved the night of Sinterklaas's visit to December 24 (Christmas Eve).

Under Swedish rule, children had been educated by their parents or by ministers who also served as teachers. The Dutch, a people who loved education, sent the first schoolmaster who wasn't also a minister into Delaware. His name was Evert Pietersen, and he arrived at New Amstel in 1657. Schoolmaster Pietersen was soon in charge of twenty-five pupils. Other Dutch and Swedish teachers arrived later.

A colonial schoolmaster

A colonial slave market in the 1600s

The Dutch who were involved in slave trading, were the first people to bring large numbers of slaves from Africa and other countries into Delaware. In the summer of 1664, just before the English seized control of Dutch lands in America, more than seventy black slaves were shipped into Delaware.

The Swedes had brought only a few slaves into Delaware. One of them was "Black Anthony," and he was a special servant to Governor Printz.

Peter Stuyvesant surrenders New Amsterdam to the English.

Chapter VI

Early English Rule: 1664–1704

Map of the lower Delaware River

New Sweden and New Netherland went the way of the weak in the struggle, which only the stronger survive.

Last sentence of The Dutch and Swedes on the Delaware: 1609–64 *by Christopher Ward*

THE ENGLISH CONQUEST OF DELAWARE

By the early 1660s the Delaware portion of New Netherland was home to only about 1,000 colonists. The Dutch had experienced almost as much trouble as the Swedes in getting people to settle in America. Those who did move to the new country settled mainly in or near New Amsterdam because of the opportunities it offered.

Meanwhile, England, which claimed the right to colonize America based on the 1497 voyage of John Cabot, had gradually taken over most of the East Coast of what is now the United States. By 1663 England controlled Maine (then part of Massachusetts), New Hampshire, Massachusetts, Rhode Island, Connecticut, Maryland, Virginia, and Carolina (not yet separated into North and South Carolina). Like missing pieces in a jigsaw puzzle, three areas along the East Coast were not yet under English control. One was Georgia, which the English didn't settle until 1733. The second was Florida, which was firmly under Spain's control. The third was the Dutch territory of New Netherland which, by 1663, comprised parts of modern-day New York, Delaware, New Jersey, and Pennsylvania.

From time to time European nations claiming the same land in various parts of the world divided it up in friendly deals. But between 1652 and 1674 England and The Netherlands fought three sea wars, so a friendly deal concerning North American lands was out of the question. Whichever country could claim and hold New Netherland by force would control it. And when it came to force, England had an overwhelming advantage in North America.

As of 1664, New Netherland had only about 10,000 colonists, most of them in present-day New York, and Governor Stuyvesant had fewer than five hundred soldiers at his command. England at that time had about 100,000 colonists in America and could raise an army of many thousands.

Charles II, who had become king of England in 1660, thought of a way to seize New Netherland with little effort on his part. In 1664 he gave New Netherland as a gift to his brother, James, the Duke of York. Since the king didn't have New Netherland in his possession, there was a "string" attached. To obtain his gift, James had to take it away from the Dutch. That wouldn't be very difficult, since James commanded the English Navy.

King Charles II

In May 1664, James sent out three hundred men in a fleet of warships under Colonel Richard Nicolls to seize New Netherland. That August, the ships reached New Amsterdam and aimed their guns at the Dutch colonial capital. Colonel Nicolls sent a message to Governor Stuyvesant ordering him to surrender New Netherland to England.

One of Peter Stuyvesant's best traits was that he tried to avoid bloodshed. In 1655 after conquering New Sweden without a fight he had returned home to find a hundred of his people dead and much of his colony in ruins from the Peach War. But since the Peach War had been started by a colonist, and the Native Americans held many of his people prisoner, Stuyvesant had not sought revenge. Instead he made peace with the Indians, arranged for the release of many of the prisoners, and began rebuilding his colony.

Faced with the demand that he surrender New Netherland, though, Stuyvesant wanted to fight. He was about the only person in New Amsterdam who felt that way. Even Stuyvesant's seventeen-year-old son joined ninety-two other people in sending him a petition asking that he surrender. "I had rather be carried to my grave!" Stuyvesant said, but he went along with his people's wishes and once again avoided bloodshed. Old "Stubborn Pete" signed the papers turning New Netherland over to the English on September 8, 1664.

Colonel Richard Nicolls sent an Englishman named Sir Robert Carr down from New Amsterdam to claim the Delaware region. Carr reached New Amstel on September 30, 1664. The previous year, the City of Amsterdam had taken over all of Dutch-held Delaware, and so there was no longer a separate City Colony and Company Colony. The Dutch governor of Delaware at the time was Alexander D'Hinoyossa, an unpopular man who had been accused of seizing the colonists' property and of letting criminals who were his friends go free.

Sir Robert Carr ordered D'Hinoyossa to surrender. Although the people of New Amstel wanted him to give up, D'Hinoyossa did not follow in

Peter Stuyvesant's footsteps. Instead he chose to fight the English even though there was no chance to win.

The English fired on the fort and stormed it, killing three Dutch soldiers and wounding ten. The English then stole or destroyed a great deal of property in Delaware, most of it belonging to Dutch officials or the Dutch government. The English seem to have done this partly to punish D'Hinoyossa for not surrendering and partly out of greed. Despite this loss of property, many of the people of Delaware welcomed English rule as a relief from the tyrant D'Hinoyossa.

Thus in 1664 Dutch attempts to colonize America came to an end, as New Netherland passed into English hands. The Delaware region had been under Dutch control for only nine years. English rule would last (with one short, strange interruption) until the end of colonial times.

There were the usual name changes when the English took over, just as had occurred with the Dutch takeover of New Sweden. The largest part of the territory was named New York, in honor of James, the Duke of York. The town of New Amsterdam became New York City. Another part of the territory was named New Jersey for the Isle of Jersey in the English Channel. Delaware was, as we know, named for the English Lord De La Warr who had helped save the Virginia Colony fifty-four years earlier. The town of New Amstel became New Castle. New Castle, which was Delaware's capital during the years of English rule, was named either for the English Earl of Newcastle or for the town in northern England called Newcastle upon Tyne.

Delawareans who swore loyalty to the new ruling country were allowed to go on with life as usual. Most people did this. By 1664 some long-time colonists had lived under three flags—the Swedish, the Dutch, and now the English. They were to switch flags twice more because of "short, strange interruptions."

In the summer of 1673, while England and The Netherlands were fighting one of their wars, a Dutch fleet sailed to America and reclaimed New York, New Jersey, and Delaware. For a short time the Dutch flag flew once more over Delaware, and New Castle returned to being New Amstel. But a few months later, in 1674, New York, New Jersey, and Delaware were returned to England by a peace treaty the English made with the Dutch. This time Delaware remained under English control for just over a hundred years.

In 1673, a Dutch fleet reclaimed New York, New Jersey, and Delaware.

DELAWARE BECOMES A TERRITORY
OF PENNSYLVANIA

In its first few years as an English colony, Delaware was ruled by the governor of New York. During those years English settlers from New Jersey, Maryland, Virginia, New York, and England came to live in Delaware alongside the Swedes, the Dutch, and the Finns. They didn't exactly pour in, though. By 1680 Delaware's population was still not much above 1,000, placing it ahead of only Pennsylvania among England's twelve American Colonies. (Georgia wasn't colonized yet.)

William Penn

George Fox

However, during the 1680s, Pennsylvania experienced such rapid growth that by 1690 it had nearly ten times as many people as Delaware. By then Delaware had become a territory of Pennsylvania, through an interesting chain of events.

It happened that Charles II, the king who had cleverly gotten his brother to seize New Netherland, owed a large debt to a young Englishman named William Penn. Penn was a leading member of a new Christian group called the Religious Society of Friends. Although the Friends were a peaceful people to whom spiritual values were more important than wealth or power, they angered the king and many other officials in England. For one thing, they had abandoned England's official religion—the Church of England. Also, since they considered everyone equal in God's eyes, the Friends treated the rich and famous no differently than they treated beggars. In addition, the Friends annoyed other English people by refusing to fight in the army.

Opponents of the Religious Society of Friends laughingly called them "Quakers" because their founder, George Fox, had once said that people should "tremble at the word of the Lord." Today the Friends are still often called Quakers, but not

In the 1600s, the Quakers were persecuted by the
English authorities.

in the mocking way that the name was used in
the 1600s. Between 1661 and the early 1680s,
about 15,000 of these peace-loving people were
jailed, and about 500 of them died as a result of
their mistreatment.

William Penn was jailed several times for
preaching and writing books promoting freedom
of worship for the Quakers. Each time Penn was

released from jail, he went back to writing books and preaching in the London streets. All of this embarrassed King Charles II because William Penn's father, Admiral Penn, had been a good friend to the royal family. In fact, Admiral Penn had lent Charles II a large sum of money. After the Admiral died in 1670, the king owed the money to William Penn.

The Penn coat of arms

By the late 1670s, William Penn felt that England offered "no hope" for religious freedom. In 1680 he asked King Charles II to repay his debt with American land instead of money. King Charles II knew that New Sweden and New Netherland had failed mainly because they hadn't had enough people to develop and defend their land. He realized that the secret to holding onto American colonies was populating them.

By the early 1680s there was a large region between New York, New Jersey, and Maryland that was claimed by England but had very few English colonists. When William Penn asked Charles II for American land instead of money, the king saw that he could kill four birds with one stone. He could populate the empty area between New York, New Jersey, and Maryland. He could get rid of William Penn. He could get rid of thousands of other Quakers whom Penn wanted to send to

America. And he could settle his debt to the Penn family.

After hassling a little with his brother, James, to whom he had given this same land a few years earlier, Charles granted the empty region between New York, New Jersey, and Maryland to William Penn in 1681. The king named this new colony *Pennsylvania* (meaning "Penn's Woods") in honor of William's father, Admiral Penn.

William Penn looked at the map and saw one problem. Pennsylvania was cut off from the Atlantic Ocean by the small Delaware Colony. Penn decided that he wanted Delaware added to his Pennsylvania grant so that he would have an outlet to the sea. In 1682 the Duke of York agreed to turn Delaware over to Penn. Delaware then went from being a territory of New York to a territory of the Penn family, which it remained until the Revolutionary War. Delaware was known as Pennsylvania's "Three Lower Counties on the Delaware," because it was made up of three counties located a short way from Pennsylvania on the Delaware River. Sometimes it was also called Pennsylvania's "Territory on the Delaware."

Until the Revolutionary War began, the man appointed by the Penns to govern Pennsylvania also ruled Delaware. However, the people of Penn-

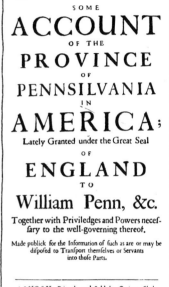

SOME
ACCOUNT
OF THE
PROVINCE
OF
PENNSILVANIA
IN
AMERICA;
Lately Granted under the Great Seal
OF
ENGLAND
TO
William Penn, &c.
Together with Priviledges and Powers necessary to the well-governing thereof.

Made publick for the Information of such as are or may be disposed to Transport themselves or Servants into those Parts.

LONDON: Printed, and Sold by Benjamin Clark Bookseller in George-Yard Lombard-street, 1681.

Title page of a book written to persuade colonists to move to Pennsylvania

Seal of Penn's colony

sylvania and Delaware also had some self-government. Penn allowed the two colonies to have an Assembly that met in Philadelphia. The total number of representatives sent by Delaware's three counties equaled the number sent by Pennsylvania's three counties. Delawareans accepted this system for about twenty years. Only after it became obvious that Pennsylvania would have many more than three counties—and would therefore have many more representatives—did Delaware win the right to have its own legislature.

Two noteworthy events shaped Delaware's borders during its first years as a territory of the Penn family. Delaware's northern boundary is as round as a penny. This occurred because William Penn's 1682 land grant stated that Delaware's northern border should be a partial circle twelve miles north of New Castle. The Twelve Mile Circle, as it is called, is still the boundary between northern Delaware and southeastern Pennsylvania.

The other major event concerning Delaware's borders nearly cost the little colony its existence. In 1632 England's King Charles I had granted the Maryland region to Cecil Calvert, the second Lord Baltimore. So by the time William Penn took control of Pennsylvania and Delaware, the Calvert family protested. They had been claiming that Delaware was theirs for years. On several occasions, supporters of the Calverts had nearly fought with Delawareans over the ownership of the land. When William Penn arrived in America in late 1692 to govern Pennsylvania and Delaware, he met with the Calverts several times to discuss their dispute over Delaware. Finally, the third Lord Baltimore and William Penn both went to England to argue their cases.

Cecil Calvert

Penn's lawyers used the same argument that the Dutch had used with the Calverts back in the 1650s in a dispute over Delaware. The second Lord Baltimore had received his grant to Maryland back in June 1632. The grant stated that Lord Baltimore could only settle land that had been previously unoccupied except by Indians. The short-lived Dutch settlement of Zwaanendael had been in existence at that time. Since the Delaware region had been occupied by Europeans when Lord Baltimore received his grant, he wasn't entitled to add it to Maryland!

William Penn's argument won out over Lord Baltimore's. It was ruled in England that the Penn family was entitled to Delaware. Although it lasted just a short time, Zwaanendael has been called "the cradling of a State" because it prevented the

Calverts from making Delaware part of Maryland.

NEW TOWNS

William Penn welcomed not only Quakers but also members of many other religions to Pennsylvania. And he welcomed not only English people, but also people from Germany, The Netherlands, Wales, and other countries. Some of these people settled in Delaware, and the little colony's population slowly increased. The

Penn's colonists arrive on the Delaware River.

newcomers lived much like the other Delawareans. They built farms where they grew wheat, rye, corn, and barley and raised cows, pigs, and sheep.

Towns developed in areas where a number of families settled. In the early 1680s, John and Richard Walker (who were probably brothers) bought some land in central Delaware from some Native Americans. The Walkers paid three coats, twelve bottles of liquor, and four handfuls of gunpowder for this land. In 1683 William Penn ordered that a town named Dover be built in this area. By the year 1700 Dover had a courthouse and a prison. Many years later, in 1777, Dover became Delaware's capital, which it still is today.

By 1700, Lewes, where Zwaanendael had been located, was growing. Also settled by 1700 were Newark, which today is the home of the University of Delaware, and Christina, which had just a few families at the time but later grew into the city of Wilmington. New Castle, with a population of a few hundred people, was still Delaware's most important town as of the year 1700.

DELAWARE GETS ITS OWN LEGISLATURE

Compared to the people in most of the other American colonies, Pennsylvanians and Delawareans had been granted a great deal of freedom by William Penn. The great Quaker was shocked when instead of thanking him, his people asked for even more say in their government. Penn even coined a word for it. He said that Pennsylvanians and Delawareans were too "governmentish," meaning too concerned with politics.

Delaware had a special problem. It was being dwarfed by Pennsylvania, its parent colony. By 1700 Delaware had about 2,500 people while Pennsylvania had about 20,000. Both colonies were still equally represented in the Assembly, because both still had three counties. But Delawareans saw the day approaching when Pennsylvania would have much more power in the Assembly because it would have many more counties to send representatives. (They were justified in their fears. Pennsylvania now has sixty-seven counties while Delaware still has only three.) As they were increasingly outnumbered, the Delawareans would have less and less voice in the government.

Delawareans also were upset about several other matters. One of them involved piracy. From time to time pirates sailed up to the Delaware coast and raided towns. For example, in the late summer of 1698 about eighty pirates raided the

A pirate captain receives chests of plundered treasure (left). A pirate ship sinks a merchant vessel (right) at sea.

town of Lewes, stealing money, clothes, and jewels from homes and killing livestock. The government in Philadelphia offered Delaware little protection from the pirates. It wasn't that Pennsylvanians didn't want to protect their little "Territory on the Delaware." It was just that part of the legislature was dominated by the Quakers, a people who hated making plans that might lead to fighting.

Another problem was that agents for Lord Baltimore (who still wanted Delaware) tried now and then to make Delawareans pay taxes, sometimes at gunpoint. The government in Philadelphia didn't do much to stop this either. A more practical problem was the fact that the Pennsylvania-Delaware legislature met in Philadelphia. In an emergency, days could be lost sending messages between Philadelphia and Delaware.

One of the last straws for Delawareans came in 1701. That year, the king asked William Penn to raise money from Pennsylvania and Delaware to help New York defend itself against the French and the Indians. Penn passed this request on to the legislature. Delawareans resented the fact that some Pennsylvanians seemed more willing to help powerful New York than their little colony. Soon after that, nine Delaware lawmakers walked out of the legislature in Philadelphia.

In 1701 Penn set up a system by which Delaware and Pennsylvania could have a peaceful legislative separation. If either colony wanted a separation anytime during the next three years, Delaware could form its own government. By mutual agreement Delaware withdrew from the legislature in Philadelphia in 1704. The little colony created a legislature of its own, which first met in New Castle in November 1704. New Castle remained Delaware's capital until 1777.

The courthouse square in New Castle, Delaware

Technically, Pennsylvania's governor still had final say over virtually all matters concerning Delaware, and the little colony officially remained a territory of the Penn family until the Revolutionary War. But, for the most part, the Penns and their appointed governors of Pennsylvania and Delaware left Delaware alone.

WILLIAM PENN (1644–1718)

William Penn was born in London, England. His father, Admiral Penn, wanted his son to join the British navy or become a lawmaker. But when William was about ten he had an experience that made him more like his very religious mother. While alone in his room, William suddenly felt God's presence. Not long after that, on a visit to Ireland, William heard Quaker Thomas Loe preach. Loe's words about how everyone had God inside them reminded William of his own religious experience. William began to think about becoming a Quaker.

Still hoping that he would become a lawmaker, Admiral Penn sent sixteen-year-old William to Oxford University. William was brilliant, but he rebelled against the rule that students had to attend Church of England services. Instead of doing this, he held prayer meetings with some friends. First he was fined for his actions, but in 1662 when he was not yet eighteen years old he was kicked out of Oxford.

Admiral Penn kept trying to rid William of his ideas about religion. He whipped William. He sent him on a long European trip in the hope that meeting other rich people would make William more interested in worldly pleasures. He sent William to law school for a while, and to Ireland to oversee the family property there. Over time, William met more people with the same ideas as himself, and by the age of twenty-two he had become a Quaker.

It was dangerous to be a Quaker in England in those years. Thousands of English Quakers were imprisoned and tortured between the 1660s and the 1680s. William Penn was jailed a number of times—once in the famous Tower of London—for preaching and writing about Quaker beliefs. In 1670, while he was on trial for preaching in the London streets, William Penn helped bring about a change in England's laws. When the judges told the jury to find him guilty of having disturbed the peace, Penn said that judges shouldn't tell the jury how to vote. The jury agreed and found Penn not guilty. For this the jurors were themselves fined and jailed, but they sued the judges and won. This helped establish the principle that accused people have a right to a trial by an unbiased jury.

A month after William was acquitted in this case, his father died. William inherited a fortune and also the king's IOU for the money he owed Admiral Penn. In 1681 William was given Pennsylvania to settle this debt, and the next year he was given Delaware also.

Although William Penn continued to live in England, he visited his American colonies twice for a total of about four years. On his first visit, Penn was welcomed by Delawareans when he landed in New Castle in October 1682. He soon continued up the Delaware River to the town he

The trial of William Penn

was building as Pennsylvania's new capital. Penn called this town *Philadelphia* (meaning "Brotherly Love" in Greek) because he wanted the Pennsylvanians and Delawareans to live in love and peace. While in America, he spent most of his time in Pennsylvania.

William Penn was loved not only by the colonists but also by the Native Americans. He was one of very few colonial leaders who treated them as his equals. Penn probably would have preferred spending the rest of his life in Pennyslvania, but he had to return to England in 1701 to settle a problem over the ownership of his American lands. Penn never again returned to America. Because he was such a trusting soul, he was cheated in business deals and spent a year in debtors' prison in his later years. This great man, who had done so much to colonize America and to promote the idea of freedom of religion, died in England at the age of seventy-three.

Chapter VII

Years of Steady Growth: 1705–1760

We are independent of them [Pennsylvania], which we esteem no small part of our Happiness, and will ever assert & support that Independency.

    Statement by Delaware lawmakers in the 1750s affirming their colony's independence from Pennsylvania

Between 1705 and the 1760s Delaware was generally left alone by both Pennsylvania and England. In fact, Connecticut and Rhode Island may have been the only two colonies that were as independent as Delaware. In a typical year the Pennsylvania governor visited Delaware just once or twice. The rest of the year he was represented by a deputy governor, who generally did not interfere in Delaware politics, either. John Evans, a deputy governor who *did* interfere, was recalled by William Penn in 1708 after Delawareans complained about him.

Delaware was fortunate in another way. It was not affected very much by four wars that England fought against France between 1689 and 1763 for control of North America. Since most of the Native Americans who took part in the fighting helped the French, these four conflicts are sometimes called the French and Indian Wars. Some historians refer to them as the Colonial Wars.

Now and then, French vessels attacked American ships in Delaware Bay during these wars, but unlike such colonies as Massachusetts and New York, there were no major battles or Indian raids inside Delaware. However, in 1709 the French raided the town of Lewes. The French took four prisoners, but soon traded them for corn and sheep. Delaware men drove off the French when they tried to raid Lewes again a short time later. Despite the fact that Delaware wasn't hurt much by the French and Indian Wars, the colony contributed to the English victory by providing men, food, and money for the fighting forces.

Swedish settlers on the Delaware

Because Delaware was hardly touched by the French and Indian Wars and was left alone by outsiders, it prospered. Between 1705 and 1760 the colony's population increased from about 3,000 to about 35,000 people. As prosperity came to the colony, Delawareans improved their way of life. Instead of log cabins, many people built brick

Dutch stone house in New Castle

and stone houses, some of which are still standing. And instead of raising only enough crops to feed their families, some Delawareans sold such products as flour and lumber to other colonies, islands in the Caribbean Sea, and Europe.

Delaware was also home to an increasing number of people who had not come there voluntarily—the black slaves. By 1740 about 1,000 slaves lived in Delaware. Only two colonies—Georgia, which had just been founded in 1733, and New Hampshire—had fewer slaves than Delaware. Virginia, with about 60,000 slaves, had the most. But the fact that Delaware had fewer slaves than most of the other colonies didn't help those 1,000 oppressed people.

Throughout the American Colonies, white people feared that the slaves would revolt. This was less of a threat in Delaware—where most owners only had one or two slaves to help with the farming and housework—than it was in most other colonies. Nevertheless, during the early 1700s Delaware passed special laws concerning its slaves. For example, slaves were denied a jury trial in certain cases, given harsher penalties than whites for the same crimes, and were

The whipping post and the pillory were some of the harsh punishments for wrongdoing.

forbidden to meet in large numbers. Some of the "black laws" applied not only to slaves, but also to the few free African Americans who lived in Delaware.

Delaware also had hundreds of white people called indentured servants who were like slaves in some ways. The indentured servants were poor Europeans whose passage to America had been paid for by wealthy Americans. In return, the indentured servants had to work for these people for about five years. Like the slaves, the indentured servants worked long hours at difficult jobs for no pay, but they had one big advantage. When their five-year indenture ended, the servants were free and could build homes of their own. Slaves were generally slaves for life, and their children were also slaves.

Many of Delaware's indentured servants were Scotch-Irish or Irish people. Both these groups were from Ireland, an island that lies less than a hundred miles west of England. England began occupying Ireland in the 1500s. The English, who were Protestants, tried to destroy the Catholic religion by outlawing Catholic services and by killing Irish-Catholic priests. The English also moved some Irish-Catholics off their ancestral lands and in their place settled Protestants from

England and nearby Scotland. The Protestants who were transplanted from Scotland to northern Ireland were known as the Scotch-Irish.

The Scotch-Irish suffered from unfair taxes and religious restrictions imposed by Ireland's English rulers. The Irish-Catholics, who were much worse off, hated the English for trying to wipe out their religion and way of life.

Starting in the early 1700s, large numbers of Scotch-Irish people left northern Ireland and moved to America, often as indentured servants. Philadelphia was their main destination, but some went to live in northern Delaware's New Castle County. Although the Irish-Catholics didn't come to the United States in huge numbers until the 1840s and 1850s, some of them settled in Delaware as indentured servants during the 1700s. Because of their hostility toward England, the Scotch-Irish and Irish Americans played important roles when the thirteen colonies rebelled against English rule in the 1770s.

The English Quakers made a big contribution to Delaware by developing the town that grew into the state's largest city. Until the 1730s, only a few people lived around what became Wilmington. Called Fort Christina by the Swedes and Fort Altena by the Dutch, the area was at first called

A Quaker
worship service

Christina by the English. Swedish and Dutch people still lived in the region under English rule. In 1698–99 Swedish people in Christina had built Old Swedes Church—now a famous landmark and one of the oldest Protestant churches still in use in the United States. Nonetheless, Christina still wasn't much of a town by the late 1720s.

In 1727 a Swedish man named Andrew Justison bought a large tract of land in the Christina area. Justison's daughter married Thomas Willing, an English merchant. During the early 1730s, Justison and Willing began laying out a town on the land Justison had bought. At first this town was called Willingtown, for Thomas Willing. Justison and Willing sold lots in the town to other colonists, and by 1735 Willingtown had about twenty homes.

A prominent Quaker couple named Elizabeth and William Shipley lived in nearby Pennsylvania. The Quakers did not have ministers. Instead, any Quaker who felt inspired by God could speak to the congregation. Elizabeth Shipley sometimes did this, and became famous as one of the few female preachers in colonial America. Elizabeth also felt that God spoke to people in dreams. When she passed through the Willingtown area on a trip, Elizabeth realized that she had dreamed about a place much like this. She and William decided to move to Willingtown.

In 1735 Elizabeth and William Shipley bought a large piece of land in Willingtown. On the corner of Fourth and Shipley streets they built a mansion for themselves. They also sold some land to other Quakers who settled in Willingtown. By the late 1730s so many Quakers lived in Willingtown that people called it a "Quaker town."

Thomas Willing and William Shipley soon began arguing about where the town market should be located. Their dispute grew so bitter that eventually the Penn family had to help settle it. The argument seems to have contributed to a change in the town's name. William Shipley wasn't pleased that the town was named for his enemy, Thomas Willing. To solve the problem without making a major name change, officials in England decided to change the town's name to Wilmington, for a friend of the Penns called the Earl of Wilmington.

A major reason for Wilmington's growth was its location at the place where the Christina and Brandywine rivers meet the Delaware River. Water was the main means of transportation in colonial days, so most of the larger towns were built along the ocean or a river. Water power was used to turn wheels that ground wheat into flour.

Wilmington, Delaware

Thanks to its water power, Delaware—and especially the Wilmington region—became a major flour-milling center of colonial times. Along the Brandywine River a high-quality flour called Brandywine Superfine was produced. Millers and merchants from the Wilmington region sold Delaware flour in Philadelphia and also to many foreign cities.

The many sawmills that had been built in Delaware by the mid-1700s were also located along rivers. This enabled logs to be floated down to the sawmills. There they were cut into the lumber that went into building Delaware's new towns and farms.

Towns often grew up around sawmills, flour mills, and other kinds of mills in early America. Throughout the country today, towns with the word "mill" in them (sometimes "mil" for short) were usually the site of some kind of mill long ago. Among such towns in Delaware are Milford, Millville, and Milton in the southern part of the state and Milltown in the north not far from Wilmington.

A young colonial girl helps her mother prepare dinner.

Chapter VIII

Life in Colonial Delaware in the Early 1760s

They [the Delaware colonists] ate their own beef, pork, and poultry, along with wild game, fruits, and butter and cheese of their own making, and they grew wheat and corn enough at least for their own needs. Milk, cider, beer, and peach or apple brandy were their beverages....

From Colonial Delaware: A History *by John A. Munroe*

By 1760 Delaware was home to about 35,000 people. Only Georgia, the newest of the thirteen colonies, had fewer people than Delaware. But what Delaware lacked in numbers, it made up in variety. Besides the English (who made up about half the population), Delaware was home to Swedish, Dutch, Finnish, German, Irish, Scotch-Irish, Scottish, French, and African people. Delaware had a much larger proportion of Swedish people—about 10 percent of its population—than any other American colony at that time.

Farmers working with a horse-drawn plow

Even the chickens lived in log cabins.

Many of the differences between the people of these varied backgrounds had disappeared by 1760. The old country languages were used less and less, as the young people learned English. There were also many marriages between people of differing backgrounds. In addition, all the Delawareans, except the slaves and indentured servants, faced common problems and had a similar way of life.

By 1760, Wilmington had passed New Castle as Delaware's largest town—a rank it has retained ever since. Wilmington may have had a little over 2,000 people, New Castle about 2,000, and Dover and Lewes about 1,000 each. The towns had a kind of "downtown" area with a few shops and public buildings. Most people, though, lived on farms several miles from the downtown area.

Delaware differed from the other American colonies in one important way. The other colonies generally had thousands of very poor families as well as several very rich people among their inhabitants. Few Delawareans of the 1760s were very rich, and, aside from the slaves and indentured servants, few were very poor. Most Delawareans lived on small farms where they grew corn and wheat and raised cows, chickens, and pigs to feed themselves. Even Delawareans who worked in flour mills, sawmills, and tanneries generally had farms where they produced most of their food.

Bartering (trading) was a popular way for colonial families to obtain the things they needed. A family that had cows but no chickens would trade milk for eggs with a family that had chickens but no cows. As the Native Americans had done, the Delaware colonists obtained some of their food by hunting, fishing, and gathering berries and nuts.

Baking in a bake-kettle

Today, most Americans eat their biggest daily meal in the early evening and call it "dinner." In colonial times this meal was called "supper" but was the day's lightest meal. The reason for this was that the colonists went to bed early, and didn't need much nighttime energy. Their largest meal was breakfast, followed by the noon meal, which they called "dinner." The colonists cooked their food in big pots hung over the fireplace, which also provided heat and light at night.

Water was not a popular drink, because it was widely thought to be unhealthy. The Delaware colonists drank beer, alcoholic cider, brandy, milk, and tea. Children as well as adults often drank beer in those days.

A few Delawareans bought fancy clothes from

Colonial women made all the family's clothes.

Philadelphia merchants, and Delaware had some tailors and shoemakers of its own. Most people, though, made their own clothes out of wool, deerskin, and other materials at hand.

Some people think that colonial times were the "good old days," but in many ways they were the "bad old days." For one thing, many diseases that are now prevented by "shots" or cured with a few spoonfuls of medicine were terrible killers back then. Families often had eight or more children in colonial days because parents expected to lose several of their children to disease.

A lack of educational opportunity was another of Delaware's drawbacks in the 1760s. There were a number of church and private schools in Delaware, especially among the Quakers. In addition, some wealthier families hired tutors for their children, or packed them off to school in Philadelphia, Boston, or England. However, Delaware had no public schools as of the 1760s, and was behind Massachusetts and several other colonies in education. On many legal papers preserved from colonial Delaware, people made marks, such as crosses, because they did not know how to sign their names.

This lack of education among Delawareans was a big reason why the colony was slow in developing newspapers. The first successful newspaper in colonial America—*The Boston News-Letter*—had been founded in the Massachusetts capital in 1704. Delaware's neighbor, Pennsylvania, had founded its first newspaper in its capital city of Philadelphia in 1719. By 1760 Georgia, New Jersey, and Delaware were the only three colonies that hadn't yet founded newspapers. Georgia's first paper wasn't published until 1763, and New Jersey's first paper came a few years later in 1777. It appears that Delaware may have been the last colony to have its own newspaper, but we cannot be certain about that.

In 1761 a Philadelphian named James Adams arrived in Wilmington and soon announced that in 1762 he would publish a newspaper, the *Wilmington Courant*. Unfortunately, no copies of this paper exist today, so we don't know if James Adams carried out his plan. Delaware's first known newspaper, the *Delaware Gazette*, didn't begin publication in Wilmington until 1785, at the end of colonial times.

What was so important about newspapers? For one thing, starting in the mid-1760s many newspapers printed articles about unfair British taxes. This stirred up anger against the mother country among Americans and helped set the stage for the

Revolutionary War. Also, as Americans read about events in the other colonies, they began to feel that they were one people, and that perhaps they should join together into one country.

Delaware wasn't completely without newspapers, though. Visitors to Philadelphia brought copies of Ben Franklin's *Pennsylvania Gazette* back to Delaware, and newspapers from other towns were also brought into the little colony. This meant that the news, which was usually a few days old by the time it was printed in the newspaper, was even older by the time it reached Delaware. Still the newspapers from other colonies were better than nothing. Since most Delawareans couldn't read, often an educated person would read the newspaper aloud to a crowd of listeners.

The Delawareans of the 1760s enjoyed some kinds of entertainment that weren't much different from our own. Fairs that resemble our county and state fairs were held at several places in Delaware in the spring and the fall. Food was sold at these fairs. There was music and dancing, and sometimes entertainment by acrobats and jugglers.

Families also took turns hosting parties where people danced and socialized. Quilting and sewing

Women got together
at sewing bees.

bees were among the women's favorite ways of
combining work with pleasant company. Card-
playing, wrestling matches, and shooting contests
were among the men's favorite pastimes. Some
Delaware men also enjoyed a brutal sport called

Men enjoyed games
such as bowling.

cockfighting in which two fighting roosters known as gamecocks fought to the death. Their owners and the onlookers bet on the outcome.

Like the rest of colonial America, Delaware was a man's world when it came to politics. White men with property or money were the only Delawareans who could vote. Women, black people, and indentured servants were excluded from voting. In colonial Delaware, casting a ballot was viewed as a duty as well as a right among the small number of eligible voters. According to a law passed in 1734, any eligible voter who didn't cast his ballot had to pay a fine.

If you ever hear someone wish for the kind of lawmakers America had in colonial times, set the record straight! It was common for politicians throughout colonial America to bribe voters with money or liquor. A minister in Dover, Delaware, reported in 1762 that for two months before elections, the candidates would invite voters to "meetings." These were just drunken get-togethers at which the candidates passed out free liquor. If colonial politicians visited us today, they would be puzzled about our anger at lawmakers who take bribes and make shady deals. Generally, colonial lawmakers had to be *extremely* dishonest before they got into trouble. Bribery and shady deals were considered a normal part of politics.

If you could go back to Delaware in the early 1760s, one of the treats would be meeting people who later became famous. It would be interesting to track down a black boy named Richard Allen. Born into slavery in Philadelphia in early 1760, Richard was sold a short time later to a Delaware farmer. However, if you visited Delaware in 1765, you might have trouble speaking to that five-year-old boy who later founded the first black church in the United States—the African Methodist Episcopal Church. Slave owners generally did not want their slaves talking to outsiders.

You would probably find it easier to meet John Dickinson, Caesar Rodney, Thomas McKean, and George Read—four men who in a few years would assist in the birth of the United States. While speaking to these four Delaware lawmakers, you would want to ask them for their autographs! Their signatures are valuable today because of the famous documents they signed later in life. The Declaration of Independence issued by the United States in July 1776 was signed by Rodney, Read, and McKean for Delaware. Dickinson and Read helped create the United States Constitution and were among the five signers for the First State.

A member of the militia prepares for war.

Chapter IX

The Revolutionary War Era: 1764–1783

We're sons of the Blue Hen, and we're game to the end!

Legendary battle cry of Delaware's soldiers during the Revolutionary War

England finally defeated France in the last of the French and Indian Wars in 1763. By doing so, England seized Canada as well as all French territory (except New Orleans) east of the Mississippi River in what is now the United States. However, England had a problem. The mother country had run up huge debts while fighting the French and the Indians and also had to pay troops to guard its new American lands.

What do lawmakers usually do when they need more money for government expenses? They raise taxes! And what do the people usually do? They moan and groan but most of them pay the taxes. Many English lawmakers of the 1760s felt that taxing the American colonists was a great way to obtain money. They figured that the Americans would complain but would consider it their patriotic duty to help England solve its money problem.

Other English lawmakers who knew more about the Americans warned that the new taxes might make them rebellious. In the end, the lawmakers who favored the new taxes won out. Between 1764 and 1773 England passed a number of laws designed to tax Americans on many goods from sugar to tea. Just as some English lawmakers had warned, these tax laws made thousands of Americans fighting mad.

A 1765 stamp

The Stamp Act, which was passed in the spring of 1765 and scheduled to take effect on November 1 of that year, was despised by the colonists. This law was designed to make Americans buy special tax stamps and place them on legal papers and even newspapers. Throughout the thirteen American colonies, people declared that "Taxation without representation is tyranny!" In other words, Americans felt that since they were not represented in the British lawmaking body called Parliament, Parliament had no right to tax them.

The most violent protests were in Massachusets, where mobs smashed buildings owned by British officials. In most places the protests were milder. In New Castle, Delaware, a jury said it would not work if the court used documents with tax stamps on them. At Lewes, a crowd forced officials to promise that they would not enforce the Stamp Act.

Meanwhile, American patriots held a big meeting called the Stamp Act Congress in New York City in October 1765. Nine colonies sent delegates to this meeting. Delaware was represented by Caesar Rodney and Thomas McKean. John Dickinson, who was closely associated with both Delaware and Pennsylvania, represented Pennsylvania at the Stamp Act Congress.

The only colony that allowed British officials to sell tax stamps was Georgia, but not many were sold there. The protests by the American public and by their delegates at the Stamp Act Congress convinced English lawmakers to repeal the Stamp Act in early 1766.

Caesar Rodney

Thomas McKean

John Dickinson

England kept pushing the Americans to the brink of war with new tax demands, however. In 1767 British lawmakers passed the Townshend Acts, which taxed tea, paint, lead, and paper that were brought into the thirteen colonies. Once again Americans protested. One of the most famous protests was a series of letters published in the *Pennsylvania Chronicle* in 1767-68. Known as the *Farmer's Letters*, they were the work of John Dickinson, who may have written them at his family mansion near Dover. Dickinson's writings and other protests helped convince the British Parliament to repeal all the Townshend taxes in 1770 except the tax on tea.

By this time it wasn't just money that England wanted from the Americans. Many people in England had begun to view the Americans as wayward children who must learn to obey the mother country. And just as parents sometimes think of ways to prod or trick their children into obeying them, England thought of a way to prod or trick the Americans into paying the tax on tea. In 1773 Parliament passed the Tea Act, which lowered the overall cost of British tea while maintaining the tax on it. People in England thought the Americans would give up their ideas about "taxation without representation" and buy the tea because it was cheaper. The world would then see that Americans would abandon their principles for the sake of a few pennies.

This strategy backfired. Instead of buying British tea, thousands of Americans brewed their own tea out of raspberry leaves, sassafras, and even catnip! They called their homemade brew "liberty tea," and referred to the British tea as "that nauseous concoction." Several colonies also held "tea parties" at which British tea was destroyed. The most famous of these, the Boston Tea Party, took place in the Massachusetts capital on December 16, 1773, when 50 men dressed as Indians dumped 340 chests of British tea into the harbor.

The Boston Tea Party, 1773

To punish Bostonians for their tea party, English officials closed the port of Boston on June 1, 1774. This put many Bostonians out of work and also caused a food shortage in the city. But Americans in other colonies sent food overland to feed Boston's people.

The trouble with England had become so serious that American leaders held a big meeting to discuss what to do. Every colony but Georgia sent delegates to this First Continental Congress, which met in Philadelphia from September 5 to October 26, 1774. Delaware lawmakers told their delegates—Caesar Rodney, Thomas McKean, and George Read—to inform Congress of Delaware's determination to defend it rights.

George Read

The First Continental Congress created a "Declaration of Rights of Americans" and sent messages to Parliament asking for fairer treatment. The delegates went home in late October 1774 with the understanding that they would return to Philadelphia in the spring if British lawmakers rejected their demands.

As it became clear that Parliament wouldn't give in, Americans disagreed about how to react. In New England—which at that time meant the colonies of Massachusetts, Connecticut, New Hampshire, and Rhode Island—many people were ready to get out the guns and cannons. But in several other colonies including Delaware, New Jersey, and Georgia, the great majority of people felt that more petitions and letters should be sent to England in an effort to work out a peaceful solution. Delaware had not suffered nearly as much as New England from British injustice, and most of its people did not think the differences with the mother country justified fighting a war.

Samuel Adams

The Second Continental Congress was scheduled to open in Philadelphia on May 10, 1775. Three weeks before then, British troops in Boston were sent across the Massachusetts countryside on two missions. They were to capture the American leaders Samuel Adams and John Hancock in Lexington. Then they were to seize American military supplies in nearby Concord.

John Hancock

For some time, towns in Massachusetts had been training emergency military forces called militia. The towns wanted to be ready in case fighting broke out. At dawn on April 19, 1775, British troops arrived in Lexington to arrest Sam Adams and John Hancock. Thanks to Paul Revere, who made a night ride from Boston to warn them, the two leaders escaped. But as Adams and Hancock made their way out of town, a small group of American militiamen fought the British

Paul Revere

The Battle of Lexington

on Lexington Green. Eight Americans were killed and ten were wounded in this Battle of Lexington, the first battle of the Revolutionary War (1775–1783). Only one of the redcoats (as the Americans called the British troops, because of the color of their uniforms) was wounded in the fighting.

News of the American defeat at Lexington spread through the countryside. Massachusetts militiamen rushed to the redcoats' next target, the town of Concord. This time the Americans had more men than the British. They beat the redcoats at Concord's North Bridge, then chased them back toward Boston, shooting at them along the way. The Americans won this Battle of

Concord, the second battle of the Revolutionary War. By the time the British reached Boston, nearly 300 of their troops had been killed or wounded, while the American losses stood at about 100 men.

We know that the battles of Lexington and Concord began the Revolutionary War. Back in the spring of 1775, though, many Americans did not yet think of themselves as being at war with Britain. They considered the Lexington and Concord battles a couple of skirmishes, and thought that the Second Continental Congress would win its demands from Britain without further bloodshed.

The retreat of the redcoats from Concord

King George III

Delaware's representatives to the First Continental Congress—Rodney, McKean, and Read—were re-elected to attend the Second Continental Congress. The three men were urged to seek ways of making peace with Britain. But in case a peaceful solution couldn't be worked out, Delaware began drilling its militia units, as did other colonies.

Soon after it opened in Philadelphia on May 10, 1775, the Second Continental Congress sent a message of peace to King George III. This paper is known as the "Olive Branch Petition," because the olive branch is an ancient symbol of peace. The Olive Branch Petition stated that the American people still felt loyal to the king, but hoped that he would treat them better, so that "harmony between [Britain] and these Colonies may be restored." This petition had been written by John Dickinson, who represented Pennsylvania at the two Continental Congresses, but it also expressed the general mood in Delaware.

George III rejected the Olive Branch Petition. Instead of making peace, the British on June 17, 1775, fought the tremendous Battle of Bunker Hill against the Americans near Boston. Because they won the hill they wanted, the English claimed victory at the Battle of Bunker Hill, even though

Massachusetts colonists watched the Battle of Bunker Hill from their housetops.

they lost a thousand men compared to four hundred casualties for the Americans. The Battle of Bunker Hill did more than prove that it was too late for a peaceful solution with Britain. It prompted many Americans to start thinking about the biggest step of all—separation from Britain.

Thomas Jefferson
writing the
Declaration of
Independence

By spring of 1776 several colonies including Virginia and North Carolina were telling their delegates to the Second Continental Congress to work for American independence. All through that spring, growing numbers of Americans decided that they should form their own country. Still, by May of 1776 almost as many Americans wanted to remain part of the British Empire as wanted to create a new nation. Delaware probably had more people who wanted to remain under British rule than favored American independence.

Congress scheduled a vote for early July of 1776 on the independence question. The rules stated that the majority of a colony's delegates had to vote for independence for that colony to choose independence. If a colony had four delegates and two voted for independence and two against it, this would count as a vote against independence.

The men of the Continental Congress didn't know how the vote would go. Like the general public, some of them favored independence and some of them opposed it. But in case the vote came out for independence, Thomas Jefferson of Virginia was asked to write a paper telling the world why America wanted to be free. Jefferson wrote this paper—the Declaration of Independence—in just a few days in late June of 1776.

On July 1, 1776—the day before the official vote—Congress held a trial vote on the independence issue. Nine colonies favored separation from Britain at that time. Pennsylvania and South Carolina were opposed. New York's delegates had been told not to vote on the issue. Delaware had a special problem.

One of the three Delaware delegates, George Read, did not think America was ready for independence. Read probably reflected his colony's majority view. Delaware's other two delegates, Thomas McKean and Caesar Rodney, were strong independence men. Unfortunately, as of July 1, Rodney was at his home in Dover after helping to put down an uprising of Delawareans who were loyal to England. Unless Rodney appeared, Delaware would not choose independence when the official vote was made on July 2.

The delegates to the Continental Congress knew that it wouldn't be good enough for nine, ten, or even twelve of the colonies to vote for independence. All thirteen colonies had to support the decision. If several colonies wanted to continue British rule while most favored independence, the colonies could end up fighting each other.

This statue of Caesar Rodney in Wilmington, Delaware, commemorates his famous ride.

Thomas McKean sent a message to Caesar Rodney saying that he was desperately needed in Philadelphia for the vote. Rodney set out for Philadelphia on the night of July 1. Stories say that he rode nearly a hundred miles through stormy weather on horseback, but he may have ridden in a carriage at least part of the way.

Rodney arrived in Philadelphia just in time to swing Delaware's vote in favor of independence. Pennsylvania and South Carolina also voted for independence on July 2, 1776, as did the nine colonies that had voted that way during the trial vote a day earlier. Although New York did not vote on July 2, it made the independence vote unanimous a few days later. To this day, Caesar Rodney's ride to Philadelphia remains the most famous incident in Delaware history.

Although he had not favored independence himself, George Read signed the Declaration along with Thomas McKean and Caesar Rodney. Perhaps he did this because he changed his mind about independence, or perhaps he was willing to go along with the majority view. The signatures of Rodney, Read, and McKean can be seen at the bottom of the fourth column from the left on the Declaration of Independence.

Now that the thirteen colonies had declared themselves the thirteen United States, the colonial governments had to be transformed into state governments. In September 1776 delegates from Delaware's three counties met at New Castle to draft the first constitution for "the Delaware State." Under this constitution, Delaware had its own governor and freed itself completely from Pennsylvania.

For independence to become a reality, the United States had to beat the British on the battlefield. Since Britain was the most powerful country in the world at the time, this would be very difficult—and some people thought it was almost impossible. In 1775 the Continental Congress had created a national army, the Continental Army, and had chosen the Virginian George Washington to lead it. Each of the thirteen states sent men to the Continental Army and also had its own local troops. Because many Delawareans still felt uneasy about fighting England, the state provided only about 3,500 soldiers. This placed Delaware at or near the bottom in the percentage of men who fought for the American side. But what the Delaware troops lacked in numbers they made up for in dedication.

According to folklore, some Delaware soldiers carried around several fighting roosters that were called the "Blue Hen's Chickens" because they had hatched from eggs of a bluish hen. The "Blue Hen's Chickens" reportedly could outfight all other gamecocks. Because Delaware soldiers fought so well, they became known as the "Blue Hen's Chickens" also. It was even said that some of them yelled, "We're sons of the Blue Hen, and we're game to the end!" as they went into battle. More than two centuries later, Delaware is still sometimes called the *Blue Hen State* and the Blue Hen chicken is the state bird.

Delaware men fought the British in New York, New Jersey, Pennsylvania, South Carolina, North Carolina, and Virginia. They also fought in the only Revolutionary War battle inside Delaware, a skirmish called the Battle of Cooch's Bridge.

Monument to the battle at Cooch's Bridge on September 3, 1777.

In late summer of 1777 a large British army under Sir William Howe marched across Delaware's northern tip on its way from Maryland to Pennsylvania. Although greatly outnumbered, some Delawareans and other American troops fought the British at Cooch's Bridge near Newark, Delaware, on September 3, 1777. The Americans hoped to stop the British advance toward Philadelphia. Although each side had about thirty men killed or wounded, the Americans lost the Battle of Cooch's Bridge. The redcoats went on to defeat George Washington's forces on September 11, 1777, in the major Battle of Brandywine, and seized Philadelphia, Pennsylvania. The day after the Battle of Brandywine, the redcoats arrived at Wilmington, Delaware, about thirty miles from Philadelphia. They seized Wilmington and captured John McKinly, the first governor of the Delaware State.

Scene from the Battle of Brandywine

By this time the British controlled the Delaware River, and Delawareans were afraid that the redcoats would capture their capital, New Castle, which lies on the river. Because of this danger, in October 1777 the Delaware state capital was moved inland to Dover, where it has been located ever since. A few months later, in early 1778,

Caesar Rodney was chosen as Delaware's governor.

The British had little interest in Wilmington except as a place to nurse men who had been wounded at the Battle of Brandywine and to store food. They left Wilmington in October 1777. John McKinly was released about a year later. Partly because he had seemed to side with his British captors, McKinly never again served as Delaware's governor.

The Americans found it much more difficult to win the Revolutionary War than to reclaim Wilmington. If not for the help of the French, who joined the American side in early 1778, the cause might have been lost. In June 1778 the British were forced to withdraw from Philadelphia. About three years later, in early 1781, Delaware troops helped the American army win battles at Cowpens, South Carolina, and at Guilford Courthouse, North Carolina.

Delaware men also took part in the last major battle of the Revolution. Called the Battle of Yorktown, it was fought in Virginia in October 1781. The Americans and the French under George Washington won the Battle of Yorktown, forcing 8,000 British troops to surrender.

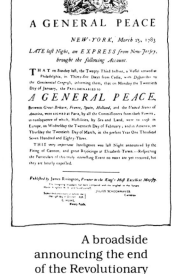

A broadside announcing the end of the Revolutionary War

The English surrender at Yorktown

The war officially ended in 1783 when the British and the Americans signed a peace treaty acknowledging the American victory. With the signing of this treaty, the thirteen American colonies passed into history. Delaware and the twelve other former colonies were now the thirteen United States of America—even in the eyes of England!

CAESAR RODNEY (1728-1784)

Caesar Rodney was born on his parents' farm near Dover, Delaware. There is no record of his attending school, but we know that his mother loved books. Caesar received his education from his parents and perhaps several traveling teachers.

Caesar Rodney

When Caesar was seventeen years old, his father died. Caesar helped raise his brother, Thomas, who was a baby at the time. Ten years later, at the age of twenty-seven, Caesar Rodney entered public life as sheriff of Kent County, Delaware. Until his death nearly thirty years later, he served Delaware in many ways. Among other things, he was a delegate from Kent County to the Delaware Colonial Assembly between 1758 and 1776.

Rodney did all this despite poor health. He had asthma, and starting in the 1760s he suffered from a cancerous tumor on his face. In 1768 he had part of the tumor removed, but his doctors couldn't cut away all of it. Although we have no portrait of Rodney, his friend John Adams of Massachusetts reported that "Caesar Rodney is the oddest looking man in the world. He is tall, thin and slender as a reed, [and] pale. His face is not bigger than a large apple, yet there is sense and fire, spirit, wit, and humor in his countenance."

Rodney was probably thin, pale, and strange-looking because of his cancer. Yet only a handful of Americans did as much for their country during the Revolutionary era as Caesar Rodney. He served in the First and Second Continental Congresses as a strong supporter of America's rights. During the Second Congress, he made his famous ride to Philadelphia to swing Delaware's vote to independence. A modest man, Rodney mentioned this ride only briefly in a letter to his brother, Thomas, on July 4, 1776:

> ... I arrived in Congress (tho detained by Thunder and Rain) time Enough to give my Voice in the matter of Independence. . . . We have now Got through with the Whole of the declaration [Declaration of Independence] and Ordered it to be printed, so that you will soon have the pleasure of seeing it. . . .

During the war Rodney helped recruit Delawareans for the Continental Army, and for a time he himself was on active duty in New Jersey. He also helped organize Delaware into a state in 1776, and served as its governor from spring of 1778 to late 1781. Unfortunately, Caesar Rodney did not have much time to enjoy the American victory because in June of 1784 his cancer finally killed him. Although he had never married, Caesar Rodney had helped raise his brother Thomas's son, Caesar Augustus Rodney, just as he had helped raise Thomas many years earlier. Thomas Rodney served as a Delaware lawmaker and judge. Caesar Augustus Rodney was Attorney General of the United States between 1807 and 1811.

THOMAS MCKEAN (1734–1817)

Thomas McKean (pronounced *Mih•Kayn*) was born into a Scotch-Irish family in Pennsylvania's Chester County, just above the Twelve Mile Circle that forms Delaware's northern border. Thomas's mother died when he was only eight years old. Thomas was sent to live at a boarding school not far from his home. The family was never reunited after that.

Thomas McKean

For seven years Thomas studied Latin, Greek, mathematics, and philosophy at the boarding school. Afterward, he studied law in nearby New Castle, Delaware, and became a lawyer at the tender age of twenty.

In those days, many lawyers rode across the countryside from courthouse to courthouse practicing their profession. Thomas McKean was a great horseback rider and eager to make his fortune. He was also very big and strong, standing well over six feet in height at a time when the average American man was probably around five feet five inches. McKean covered great distances so quickly and worked on so many cases at the same time that he sometimes seemed to be in two places at once.

McKean entered politics during the mid-1750s, and in 1762 he was elected to the Delaware Assembly from New Castle County. He was so popular that he was re-elected again and again for over fifteen years. In those days some of the American colonies had their laws written down in scattered places. In 1762, his first year in the Delaware Assembly, McKean helped compile all of Delaware's laws in one place.

A short time later, the troubles with Britain began. Like many other Scotch-Irish people, McKean firmly opposed British injustice. One British sympathizer even called him "the violent raging rebel McKean" because of his strong support of the American cause. McKean represented Delaware at the Stamp Act Congress and at the First and Second Continental Congresses. It was Thomas McKean who sent the message prompting Caesar Rodney's famous ride for independence in July 1776.

Two months after the Declaration of Independence was approved, McKean helped create Delaware's first state constitution. For a short time in 1777 he was Delaware's governor, and for a few months in 1781 he was President of the United States Congress of the Confederation. This was equivalent to being the President of the United States, but with far less power than the president had under the U.S. Constitution created in 1787.

Later in life, Thomas McKean did some of the same things for Pennsylvania that he had done for Delaware. He helped compile Pennsylvania's laws and create a state constitution. He also served as governor of Pennsylvania from 1799 to 1808. The father of eleven children by his two wives, and one of the most important of the "Founding Fathers," Thomas McKean died in Philadelphia at the age of 83.

George Washington (standing) was president of the Constitutional
Convention that met in 1787.

Chapter X

Delaware Becomes the First State!

The best [frame of government] the world has yet seen.

Thomas McKean of Delaware and Pennsylvania describing the United States Constitution

In the summer of 1776, the Continental Congress gave John Dickinson of Delaware and Pennsylvania a very important job. He was to write a set of national laws for the United States, which was just declaring its independence. The national laws Dickinson proposed would have created a strong central government that would have taken over some of the powers claimed by the thirteen new states.

At that time, few Americans wanted to strengthen the U.S. government at the expense of the states. For one thing, Americans were generally more loyal to their states than they were to the newborn nation as a whole. For another, what if a stronger U.S. government tried to tax them, as the British had tried to do?

Congress would not approve the document as Dickinson had written it. Congress watered down Dickinson's ideas until they set up a weak instead of a strong central government. In late 1777 Congress approved these Articles of Confederation, as the national laws were called. But the Articles were not to take effect until they had been approved by all thirteen states.

Aside from wanting to win the war against Britain, the thirteen states didn't agree on very much. In those early days of the country, the states argued with each other over borders, the use of rivers and ports, slavery, and many other matters. It took more than three years for all thirteen states to sign the Articles.

Unfortunately, the Articles of Confederation did a poor job of holding the nation together. This became clear after the United States won the Revolutionary War. In fact, it seemed that the country that had won its freedom from mighty Britain would crumble of its own accord.

The nation was weak in many ways. It had no president to lead it, no national courts, and no national money. The country could not pay many of its debts because its only way of raising funds was to beg the states for it. Generally the states gave the national government, called the Congress of the Confederation, less than a tenth of the money that it needed. In addition, the United States broke its promises to other nations, largely because it could not control the states.

Some of the national government's mishaps might have been funny if they weren't so pitiful. For example, in the summer of 1783 some soldiers marched to the building in Philadelphia where United States lawmakers met. The soldiers wanted the pay that they were owed by the federal government. Congress lacked the money, so what did the lawmakers do? They packed up and ran away to Princeton, New Jersey, which then replaced Philadelphia as the U.S. capital. Between 1776 and 1787 the capital was moved nine different times. Since news traveled slowly in those days, much of the time many Americans had no idea where their national capital was located!

The peace treaty ending the Revolutionary War also displayed the sad state of the national government. England and the United States agreed that the U.S. government would approve the treaty and have it back in Paris, France, by March 3, 1784. The treaty favored the United

States, so its contents posed no problem.

The problem was, at least nine states had to approve the treaty according to the Articles of Confederation. And in order for a state to approve it, at least two of its representatives had to be in Congress. By the end of 1783, only seven states were sufficiently represented in Congress. As often happened, several states had neglected to send representatives to Congress.

It took until February 14, 1784, before nine states were properly represented. Congress approved the treaty that day, but there wasn't enough time to ship it to Paris by March 3, 1784. By the time the treaty reached Paris, it was a month past the deadline. Americans were afraid that England might use this as an excuse to back out of the treaty, but fortunately this did not happen.

By 1787 Americans realized that they needed a much stronger central government. To create it, a national convention was held in Philadelphia between May and September 1787. Each colony, except Rhode Island, sent representatives to this Constitutional Convention. Delaware's representatives were John Dickinson, George Read, Jacob Broom, Richard Bassett, and Gunning Bedford, Jr.

Left to right: John Dickinson, George Read, Richard Bassett, and Gunning Bedford, Jr.

The 55 delegates to this convention created a new set of national laws called the United States Constitution. John Dickinson made an important contribution to the Constitution. He helped set up the system by which each state has a number of representatives in the U.S. House of Representatives based on population, but only two U.S. senators. Two senators per state ensured that small states such as Delaware would have as much of a voice in the Senate as the large states had.

By the time the Constitution was signed on September 17, 1787, John Dickinson had left the convention. Dickinson asked George Read to sign his name for him on the document. Besides Dickinson and Read, Delaware's other signers were Jacob Broom, Richard Bassett, and Gunning Bedford, Jr.

It had been agreed that each of the thirteen former colonies would become a state under the new Constitution when it approved the document, and that the Constitution would become the law of the land once nine of the thirteen states had approved it. The nation waited to see which state would go first. On December 3, 1787, a convention opened at Dover to decide whether Delaware would approve or reject the U.S. Constitution. The vote was made in favor of the Constitution on December 7, 1787. With that vote, little Delaware—which had been the home of the Lenni-Lenape Indians, the site of the first log cabins in America, and the birthplace of the famous patriot Caesar Rodney—became the First State!

Delaware's neighbor, Pennsylvania, became the second state five days later on December 12, 1787, while another neighbor, New Jersey, became the third state six days after that on December 18, 1787. The United States Constitution went into effect when the ninth state, New Hampshire, approved it on June 21, 1788. And finally, in May of 1790, about two-and-a-half years after Delaware had become the First State, Rhode Island became the thirteenth and last of the original states to approve the Constitution.

JOHN DICKINSON (1732-1808)

John Dickinson was born into a wealthy Quaker family in the Maryland portion of the Delmarva Peninsula. When John was eight years old, he moved with his family from their Maryland plantation into a large mansion near Dover, Delaware. John received his early education from a young Irish tutor named William Killen, who had been taken into the Dickinson home by John's father. Both teacher and pupil later made their marks in the world. Killen became Delaware's chief justice, while Dickinson became one of the most famous Americans of the Revolutionary War era.

John Dickinson

When John was twenty-one years old, he went to London, England, where he studied law for three years. Upon his return he became a prominent Philadelphia lawyer. He liked politics even more than law, though, and in 1760 his political career began with his election to the Delaware Assembly. Most of the time during the next thirty years, Dickinson worked as a public official for Delaware or Pennsylvania.

After the British began taxing Americans in the 1760s, Dickinson wrote the fourteen *Farmer's Letters* in protest. Later published in pamphlet form, these letters were among the most popular political writings that had been published in America up to that time. In these letters, Dickinson wrote that he thought America and Britain could reach an agreement but that the Americans might use force if all else failed.

Dickinson represented Pennsylvania in both the First and Second Continental Congresses. In Congress he became known as the "Penman of the Revolution" because of the important papers he wrote, including the "Declaration of the Causes of taking up Arms against England." Then in 1776 Dickinson did something that hurt his reputation among many people. He opposed American independence. Yet he stayed away from Congress on July 2, 1776, so that Pennsylvania could choose independence by a 3-2 vote.

People were puzzled by Dickinson. Why hadn't he come to Congress to vote against independence if he really opposed it? And why had he written the warlike paper about taking up arms if he opposed independence? The answers had to do with Dickinson's Quaker upbringing and personal code. As a Quaker, he hated war and wanted to settle the difficulties peacefully. But as a lawmaker he considered the majority opinion "sacred," as he once said. Since most states were voting for independence, he didn't want his personal feelings to stop Pennsylvania from doing so, too. And since Congress needed a good writer to create the declaration for taking up arms, he had done it for his country's sake.

John Dickinson's house in Wilmington, Delaware

Once independence had been declared, Dickinson realized that hopes for peace were over and so he became a soldier despite his feelings about war. Although we lack details about his career as a soldier, we know that he was at the Battle of Brandywine. He was one of only several U.S. congressmen who actually fought in the Revolution.

In 1781–82, near the end of the Revolutionary War, John Dickinson served as Delaware's governor, and from 1782 to 1785 he was governor of his other home state—Pennsylvania. In 1787 he represented Delaware at the Constitutional Convention in Philadelphia, where he did so much to create the national laws that have governed the United States for over two centuries.

Personally, John Dickinson was a warm and gentle man. Once when a friend of his died leaving his family in financial trouble, Dickinson gave the man's widow a farm in Delaware. He also helped found Dickinson College in Carlisle, Pennsylvania. John Dickinson retired from politics after Delaware and Pennsylvania approved the U.S. Constitution within five days of each other in late 1787. About twenty years later, the "Penman of the Revolution" died at the age of seventy-five in Wilmington, Delaware.

The Old State House in Dover, Delaware

A DECLARATION

By the Representatives of the

United Colonies

Of NORTH-AMERICA, now met in

General Congress

AT PHILADELPHIA,

Setting forth the CAUSES and NECESSITY

OF THEIR TAKING UP

ARMS.

A View of that great and flourishing City of BOSTON, when in its purity, and out of the Hands of the Philistines.

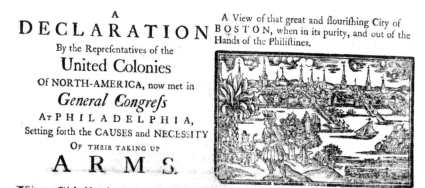

IF it was possible for Men, who exercise their Reason, to believe, that the Divine Author of our Existence intended a Part of the human Race to hold an absolute Property in, and an unbounded Power over others, marked out by his infinite Goodness & Wisdom, as the Objects of a legal Domination, never rightfully resistible, however severe and oppressive, the Inhabitants of these Colonies might at least require from the Parliament of Great Britain, some Evidence, that this dreadful Authority over them has been granted to that Body. But a Reverence for our Great CREATOR, Principles of Humanity, and the Dictates of common Sense, must convince all those who reflect upon the Subject, that Government was instituted to promote the Welfare of Mankind, and ought to be administered for the Attainment of that End. The Legislature of Great-Britain, however stimulated by an inordinate Passion for a Power not only unjustifiable, but which they know to be peculiarly reprobated by the very Constitution of that Kingdom, and desperate of Success in any Mode of Contest, where Regard should be had to Truth, Law, or Right, have at length, deserting those, attempted to effect their cruel and impolitic Purpose of enslaving these Colonies by Violence, and have thereby rendered it necessary for us to close with their last Appeal from Reason to Arms.— Yet however blinded that Assembly may be, by their intemperate Rage for unlimited Domination so to slight Justice and the Opinion of Mankind, we esteem ourselves bound by Obligations of Respect to the rest of the World, to make known the Justice of our Cause.

Our Forefathers, Inhabitants of the Island of Great-Britain, left their native Land to seek on these Shores a Residence for civil and religious Freedom. At the Expence of their Blood, at the Hazard of their Fortunes, without the least Charge to the Country from which they removed, by unceasing Labor and an unconquerable Spirit, they effected Settlements in the distant & inhospitable Wilds of America, then filled with numerous and warlike Nations of Barbarians.—Societies or Governments, vested with perfect Legislatures, were formed under Charters from the Crown, and an harmonious Intercourse was established between the Colonies and the Kingdom from which they derived their Origin.—The mutual Benefits of this Union became in a short Time so extraordinary, as to excite Astonishment: It is universally confessed, that the amazing Increase of the Wealth, Strength and Navigation of the Realm, arose from this Source; and the Minister who so wisely and successfully directed the Measures of Great Britain in the late War, publicly declared, that these Colonies enabled her to triumph over her Enemies.—Towards the Conclusion of that War, it pleased our Sovereign to make a Change in his Councils.—From that fatal Moment, the Affairs of the British Empire began to fall into Confusion, and gradually sliding from the Summit of glorious Prosperity to which they had been advanced by the Virtues and Abilities of one Man, are at length distracted by the Convulsions that now shake it to its deepest Foundations. — The new Ministry finding the brave Foes of Britain, though frequently defeated, yet still contending, took up the unfortunate Idea of granting them a hasty Peace, and of then subduing her faithful Friends.

These devoted Colonies were judged to be in such a State, as to present Victories without Bloodshed, and all the easy Emoluments of statuteable Plunder.— The uninterrupted Tenor of their peaceable and respectful Behaviour from the Beginning of Colonization, their dutiful, zealous and useful Services during the War, though so recently and amply acknowledged in the most honorable Manner by his Majesty, by the late King, and by Parliament, could not save them from the meditated Innovations.— Parliament was influenced to adopt the pernicious Project, & assuming a new Power over them, have in the Course of eleven Years, given such decisive Specimens of the Spirit and Consequences attending this Power, as to leave no Doubt concerning the Effects of Acquiescence under it. They have undertaken to give and grant our Money without our Consent, tho'

we have ever exercised an exclusive Right to dispose of our own Property; Statutes have been passed for extending the Jurisdiction of Courts of Admiralty and Vice Admiralty beyond their ancient Limits: For depriving us of the accustomed and inestimable Privilege of Trial by Jury in Cases affecting both Life and Property; for suspending the Legislature of one of the Colonies; for interdicting all Commerce of another; and for altering fundamentally the Form of Government established by Charter, and secured by Acts of its own Legislature solemnly confirmed by the Crown; for exempting the "Murderers" of Colonists from legal Trial, and in Effect, from Punishment; for erecting in a neighbouring Province acquired by the joint Arms of Great Britain and America, a Despotism dangerous to our very Existence; and for quartering Soldiers upon the Colonists in Time of profound Peace. It has also been resolved in Parliament, that Colonists charged with committing certain Offences, shall be transported to England to be tried.

But why should we enumerate our Injuries in Detail? By one Statute it is declared, that Parliament can "of Right make Laws to bind us IN ALL CASES WHATSOEVER." What is to defend us against so enormous, so unlimited a Power? Not a single Man of those who assume it, is chosen by us; or is subject to our Controul or Influence: but on the contrary, they are all of them exempt from the

Operation of such Laws, and an American Revenue, if not diverted from the ostensible Purposes for which it is raised, would actually lighten their own Burdens in Proportion, as they increase ours. We saw the Misery to which such Despotism would reduce us. We for ten Years incessantly and ineffectually besieged the Throne as Supplicants; we reasoned, we remonstrated with Parliament in the most mild and decent Language. But Administration, sensible that we should regard those oppressive Measures as Freemen ought to do, sent over Fleets and Armies to enforce them. The Indignation of the Americans was roused it is true; but it was the Indignation of a virtuous, loyal, and affectionate People. A Congress of Delegates from the united Colonies was assembled at Philadelphia, on the fifth Day of last September. We resolved again to offer an humble and dutiful Petition to the King, and also addressed our Fellow Subjects of Great Britain. We have pursued every temperate, every respectful Measure; we have even proceeded to break off our commercial Intercourse with our Fellow Subjects, as the last peaceable Admonition, that our Attachment to no Nation upon Earth should supplant our Attachment to Liberty.— This, we flattered ourselves, was the ultimate Step of the Controversy: But subsequent Events have shewn, how vain was this Hope of finding Moderation in our Enemies.

Several threatening Expressions against the Colonies were inserted in his Majesty's Speech; our Petition, though we were told it was a decent one, that his Majesty had been pleased to receive it graciously, and to promise laying it before his Parliament, was huddled into both Houses amongst a Bundle of American Papers, and there neglected. The Lords and Commons in their Address, in the Month of February last, said, "that a Rebellion at that Time actually existed within the Province of Massachusetts Bay; and that those concerned in it, had been countenanced and encouraged by unlawful Combinations and Engagements, entered into by his Majesty's Subjects in several of the other Colonies; and therefore they besought his Majesty, "that he would take the most effectual Measures to inforce due Obedience to the Laws and Authority of the supreme Legislature."— Soon after the commercial Intercourse of whole Colonies, with foreign Countries and with each other, was cut off by an Act of Parliament; by another, several of them were intirely prohibited from the Fisheries in the Seas near their Coasts, on which they always depended for their Sustenance; and large Reinforcements of Ships and Troops were immediately sent over to General Gage.

Fruitless were all the Entreaties, Arguments and Eloquence of an

In CONGRESS, July 4, 1776

The unanimous Declaration of the thirteen united States of America.

Colonial America Time Line

Before the arrival of Europeans, many millions of Native Americans belonging to dozens of tribes lived in North America (and also in Central and South America)

About 982 A.D.—Eric the Red, born in Norway, reaches Greenland during one of the first European voyages to North America

About 985—Eric the Red brings settlers from Iceland to Greenland

About 1000—Leif Ericson (Eric the Red's son) leads what is thought to be the first European expedition to mainland North America; Leif probably lands in Canada

1492—Christopher Columbus, sailing for Spain, reaches America

1497—John Cabot reaches Canada in the first English voyage to North America

1513—Ponce de León of Spain explores Florida

1519-1521—Hernando Cortés of Spain conquers Mexico

1565—St. Augustine, Florida, the first permanent European town in what is now the United States, is founded by the Spanish

1607—Jamestown, Virginia, is founded, the first permanent English town in the present-day U.S.

1608—Frenchman Samuel de Champlain founds the village of Quebec, Canada

1609—Henry Hudson explores the eastern coast of present-day U.S. for The Netherlands; the Dutch then claim parts of New York, New Jersey, Delaware, and Connecticut and name the area New Netherland

1619—Virginia's House of Burgesses, America's first representative lawmaking body, is founded

1619—The first shipment of black slaves arrives in Jamestown

1620—English Pilgrims found Massachusetts' first permanent town at Plymouth

1621—Massachusetts Pilgrims and Native Americans hold the famous first Thanksgiving feast in colonial America

1622—Native Americans kill 347 settlers in Virginia

1623—Colonization of New Hampshire is begun by the English

1624—Colonization of present-day New York State is begun by the Dutch at Fort Orange (Albany)

1625—The Dutch start building New Amsterdam (now New York City)

1630—The town of Boston, Massachusetts is founded by the English Puritans

1633—Colonization of Connecticut is begun by the English

1634—Colonization of Maryland is begun by the English

1635—Boston Latin School, the colonies' first public school, is founded

1636—Harvard, the colonies' first college, is founded in Massachusetts

1636—Rhode Island colonization begins when Englishman Roger Williams founds Providence

1638—The colonies' first library is established at Harvard

1638—Delaware colonization begins when Swedish people build Fort Christina at present-day Wilmington

1640—Stephen Daye of Cambridge, Massachusetts prints *The Bay Psalm Book*, the first English-language book published in what is now the U.S.

1643—Swedish settlers begin colonizing Pennsylvania

1647—Massachusetts forms the first public school system in the colonies

1650—North Carolina is colonized by Virginia settlers in about this year

1650—Population of colonial U.S. is about 50,000

1660—New Jersey colonization is begun by the Dutch at present-day Jersey City

1670—South Carolina colonization is begun by the English near Charleston

1673—Jacques Marquette and Louis Jolliet explore the upper Mississippi River for France

1675-76—New England colonists beat Native Americans in King Philip's War

1682—Philadelphia, Pennsylvania is settled

1682—La Salle explores Mississippi River all the way to its mouth in Louisiana and claims the whole Mississippi Valley for France

1693—College of William and Mary is founded in Williamsburg, Virginia

1700—Colonial population is about 250,000

1704—*The Boston News-Letter*, the first successful newspaper in the colonies, is founded

1706—Benjamin Franklin is born in Boston

1732—George Washington, future first president of the United States, is born in Virginia

1733—English begin colonizing Georgia, their thirteenth colony in what is now the United States

1735—John Adams, future second president, is born in Massachusetts

1743—Thomas Jefferson, future third president, is born in Virginia

1750—Colonial population is about 1,200,000

1754—France and England begin fighting the French and Indian Wars over North American lands

1763—England, victorious in the wars, gains Canada and most other French lands east of the Mississippi River

1764—British pass Sugar Act to gain tax money from the colonists

1765—British pass the Stamp Act, which the colonists despise; colonists then hold the Stamp Act Congress in New York City

1766—British repeal the Stamp Act

1770—British soldiers kill five Americans in the "Boston Massacre"

1773—Colonists dump British tea into Boston Harbor at the "Boston Tea Party"

1774—British close up port of Boston to punish the city for the tea party

1774—Delegates from all the colonies but Georgia meet in Philadelphia at the First Continental Congress

1775—**April 19:** Revolutionary War begins at Lexington and Concord, Massachusetts

       May 10: Second Continental Congress convenes in Philadelphia

       June 17: Colonists inflict heavy losses on British but lose Battle of Bunker Hill near Boston

       July 3: George Washington takes command of Continental Army

1776—**March 17:** Washington's troops force the British out of Boston in the first major American win of the war

       May 4: Rhode Island is first colony to declare itself independent of Britain

July 4: Declaration of Independence is adopted

December 26: Washington's forces win Battle of Trenton (New Jersey)

1777—**January 3:** Americans win at Princeton, New Jersey

August 16: Americans win Battle of Bennington at New York-Vermont border

September 11: British win Battle of Brandywine Creek near Philadelphia

September 26: British capture Philadelphia

October 4: British win Battle of Germantown near Philadelphia

October 17: About 5,000 British troops surrender at Battle of Saratoga in New York

December 19: American army goes into winter quarters at Valley Forge, Pennsylvania, where more than 3,000 of them die by spring

1778—**February 6:** France joins the American side

July 4: American George Rogers Clark captures Kaskaskia, Illinois, from the British

1779—**February 23-25:** George Rogers Clark captures Vincennes in Indiana

September 23: American John Paul Jones captures British ship *Serapis*

1780—**May 12:** British take Charleston, South Carolina

August 16: British badly defeat Americans at Camden, South Carolina

October 7: Americans defeat British at Kings Mountain, South Carolina

1781—**January 17:** Americans win battle at Cowpens, South Carolina

March 1: Articles of Confederation go into effect as laws of the United States

March 15: British suffer heavy losses at Battle of Guilford Courthouse in North Carolina; British then give up most of North Carolina

October 19: British army under Charles Cornwallis surrenders at Yorktown, Virginia, as major Revolutionary War fighting ends

1783—**September 3:** United States officially wins Revolutionary War as the United States and Great Britain sign Treaty of Paris

November 25: Last British troops leave New York City

1787—On December 7, Delaware becomes the first state by approving the U.S. Constitution

1788—On June 21, New Hampshire becomes the ninth state when it approves the U.S. Constitution; with nine states having approved it, the Constitution goes into effect as the law of the United States

1789—On April 30, George Washington is inaugurated as first president of the United States

1790—On May 29, Rhode Island becomes the last of the original thirteen colonies to become a state

1791—U.S. Bill of Rights goes into effect on December 15

Adams, James, 113
Adams, John, 138
Adams, Samuel, 125, **125**
African Americans, 12, 102, 116. *See also* slaves and slavery.
African Methodist Episcopal Church, 12, 117
Allen, Richard, 12, **12**, 117
Altena, 69, 70
Argall, Samuel, 33, 34
Armada, Spanish, **24**, 25
Articles of Confederation, 142, 144
Assateagues, 22
Atlantic Ocean, 5, 42, 71, 87
bartering, 111
Bassett, Richard, 144, 145
Bedford, Gunning, Jr., 144, 145, **145**
Bermuda, 33
"Black Anthony," 75
Blue Hen, **9**
Blue Hen State, 9, 134
Bombay Hook, 70
Bombay Hook National Wildlife Refuge, 13
Boston, 112, 123, 124, 125, 126, 127, 128
Boston News-Letter, The, 113
Boston Tea Party, 123, **123**, 124
Bottnyard, Sweden, 59
Brandywine, Battle of, 135, **135**, 136, 148
Brandywine Creek, 10
Brandywine River, 106, 107
Broom, Jacob, 144, 145
Bunker Hill, Battle of, 128-129, **129**
burgomasters (mayors), 71, 72
Cabot, John, 77
Calvert, Cecil (Lord Baltimore), 88, **89**, 93
Calvert family, 89
Canada, 12, 22, 119, 150
Cannon, Annie Jump, 12, **12**
Cape Henlopen, 32, 34
capital of Delaware, 13, 91, 94, 135
Carolina, 78
Carr, Robert, 80
Catholics, 102, 103
Charles I (king of England), 88
Charles II (king of England), 79, **79**, 84, 86, 87
chemical companies, 10, 11

chickens, 11
children: colonial, 112; Lenni-Lenape, 18, 19, 22
Christina (queen of Sweden), 41, 43
Christina River, 43 , 70, 106
Church of England, 26, 84, 96
City Colony, 70, 80
Civil War, 9
clothing: settlers', 48, 111-112; Lenni-Lenape, 19
cockfighting, 116, 134
Colonial Wars, 99
colonists. *See* settlers.
Company Colony, 70, 80
Concord, Battle of, 126-127, **127**
Concord, Massachusetts, 125, 126
Confederate States of America, 9
Congress of the Confederation, 143, 144
Connecticut, 7, 34, 77, 98, 124
constitution, Delaware, 133, 139
Constitution, U.S., 8, 117, 139, 145, 146, **146**, 148
Constitutional Convention, 144-145, 148
Continental Army, 8, 133, 138
Continental Congress, First, 124, 128, 138, 139, 147
Continental Congress, Second, 125, 127, 128, 130, 131, 133, 138, 139, 141, 142, 147
Cooch's Bridge, Battle of, 134, **134**, 135
corn, 17, 18, 48
Corn Dance, 22
corporate headquarters, 11
Cowpens, Battle of, 136
Declaration of Independence, 117, 130, 132, 139, 151, **151**
Declaration of Rights of Americans, 124
Delaware (people). *See* Lenni-Lenape.
Delaware Bay, 5, 13, 15, 30, 32, 33, 36, 43, 55, 61, 99
Delaware Gazette, 113
Delaware River, 5, 16, 30, 32, 33, **33**, 34, 42, 43, 44, 46, 51, 52, 55, 63, **77**, **90**, 96, 106, 135
De La Warr, Lord (Thomas West), 29, 30, **30**, 34, 82
Delmarva Peninsula, 5, 147

Denmark, 28
de Vries, David Pieterssen, 36-37, **37**, 41
D'Hinoyossa, Alexander, 80, 81
Diamond State, 9
Dickinson, John, 11-12, **11**, 117, 121, **121**, 122, 128, 141, 142, 144, 145, **145**, 147-148, **147**
Discovery (ship), 150
disease, 112
Dover, Delaware, 12, 13, 91, 110, 116, 122, 131, 135, 138, 146, 147, **149**
du Pont, E. I., 10, 11
DuPont Company, 10, **10**
Dutch. *See* settlers; explorers; Netherlands, The.
Dutch East India Company, 31, 150
Dutch West India Company, 36, 58, 70
East Indies, 31
education: colonial, 74, **74**, 112; Lenni-Lenape, 19
England, 7, 8, 12, 25-27, **26**, 39, 96, 97, 98, 102, 112, 119; colonization by, 77-82, 83, 102; Revolutionary War and, 125-127, 128-129, 133-137; taxes and, 119-124, 147. *See also* settlers.
entertainment, 114-116, **116**
Evans, John, 98
exploration: England and, 33-34; The Netherlands and, 28, 30-33
fairs, 114
farmers and farming, 11; colonial, 10, 73, 91, 100, 110, **110**, 111; Lenni-Lenape, 17, **17**, 19
Farmer's Letters, 122, 147
Finland and Finns, 46, 47, 70, 72, 83, 109
First State, 8, 117, 146
fishing: settlers and 36, 111; Lenni-Lenape and, 17, 19
Florida, 78
flour mills, 107, 111
food: colonial, 73, 111; Lenni-Lenape, 18
forests, 13
Fort Casimir, 52, 53, 55, 56-57, 61, 62, 63, 64, **65**, 67, 69
Fort Christina, 44, **44**, 46, 51, 52, 58, 59, 63, 64, 65, 66, 67, 103
Fort Elfsborg, 51
Fort Orange, 36

Fort Trefaldighet (Fort Trinity), 57, 63, 64
Fox, George, 84, **84**
France and the French, 99, 119; Revolutionary War and, 136
Franklin, Ben, 114
French and Indian Wars (Colonial Wars), 94, 99, 119
furs and fur trading, 35, **35**, 36, 46, 52
Garrett, Thomas, 12
George III (king of England), 128, **128**
Georgia, 8, 78, 100, 109, 113, 121, 124, 125
Giant Turtle, 21, **21**
gods and goddesses (Lenni-Lenape), 21
government: colonial, 88, 92-95, 98, 116-117, 120-122, 124, 133, 139, 147; of New Netherland, 71-72; state, 133; of United States, 141-146
Great Britain. *See* England.
Guilford Courthouse, Battle of, 136
Gustavus Adolphus, 28, **28**, 41
Gyllene Haj (ship), 54, 55, 61, 62
Half Moon (ship), 31, **31**, 32, 150
Hals, Frans, 28
Hancock, John, 125, **125**
Harbor of Refuge, 34
Hartford Connecticut, 36
Hollandaer, Peter, 49, 50
Hopewell (ship), 39
House of Hope, 36
House of Representatives, U.S., 145
Howe, William, 135
Hudson, Henry, 30, 31, **31**, 32, 33, 34, 39, 52,
Hudson Bay, 39
Hudson River, 33, 34, 61
Hudson Strait, 39
hunting: settlers and, 48, 111; Lenni-Lenape and, 17, 19
indentured servants, 102, 103, 110, 116
Indians. *See* Lenni-Lenape; Native Americans.
Ireland, 102
James, Duke of York, 79, **79**, 81, 87
Jamestown, Virginia, 29
Jefferson, Thomas, 130, **130**
Jersey City, New Jersey, 36
Jönsson, Anders, 54
Justison, Andrew, 104

Kalmar, Sweden, 42
Kalmar Nyckel (ship), 42, 43
Killen, William, 147
Late George Apley, The, 12
Lenni-Lenape (Delaware), 7, **14**, 15, **15**, **16**, **18**, **21**, 30, 34, 36, 146; beliefs of, 19-20; Dutch and, 37-38; religion of, 20-22; special number and, 21; village life, 16-19
Lewes, Delaware, 36, 91, 93, 99, 110, 121
Lexington, Battle of, 125-126, **126**, 127
Lexington, Massachusetts, 125, 126
Lindeström, Peter, 55, 63
Loe, Thomas, 96
log cabins, 7, 46, **47**, 99, 146
McKean, Thomas, 117, 121, **121**, 124, 128, 131, 132, 139, **139**
McKinley, John, 135, 136
Maine, 77
Manhattan Island, 42, **43**, 44, 58
manufacturing, 10, 11
Marquand, John, 12
marshes, 69-70
Maryland, 5, 7, 11, 22, 38, 77, 83, 86, 87, 88, 89, 90, 135, 147
Massachusetts, 7, 58, 77, 99, 112, 113, 120, 125
men: colonial, 115, 116, **116**; Lenni-Lenape, 17, 18, **18**, 19
Merry Adventures of Robin Hood, The, 12
Milford, Delaware, 107
militias, **118**, 125, 128
Milltown, Delaware, 107
Millville, Delaware, 107
Milton, Delaware, 107
Minuit, Peter, 42, **42**, 43, **43**, 44, 46, 49, 58, **58**
Mississippi River, 119
Muscovy Company, 39
name changes, 69, 81-82
Nanticokes, 22, **23**
Native Americans, 7, 13, **14**, 15, **15**, **16**, **18**, **21**, 22, 23, **23**, 35, **35**, 37, 42, **43**, 44, 48, 51, 52, 53, 58, 66, 71, 79, 80, 89, 91, 97; Colonial Wars and, 99. *See also* Lenni-Lenape.
Netherlands, The, 7, 25-28, **27**, 52, 58, 62, 69, 70, 78. *See also* settlers; explorers.
New Amstel, **53**, 69-70, 71, 73, 74, 80, 82

New Amsterdam, 36, 49, 54, 58, 61, 62, 66, 67, 68, 71, **72**, 73, 77, 81
Newark, Delaware, 91, 135
New Castle, Delaware, 52, 82, 91, 94, **95**, 96, 110, 121, 133, 135, 139
New Castle County, 103, 139
Newfoundland, Canada, 32
New Gothenburg, 51
New Hampshire, 7, 77, 100, 124, 146
New Jersey, 5, 8, 15, 16, 22, 34, 36, 44, 46, 51, 67, 78, 81, 83, 86, 87, 113, 125, 134, 138, 146
New Netherland, 7, 35, 36, 41, 42, 49-50, 54, 58, 62, 65, 66, **69**, 70, 77, 86; English capture of, 78-82
newspapers, 113, 114
New Sweden, 7, **14**, 46-49, 50-57, 58, 59, 61-68, 79, 81, 86
New York (state and colony), 7, 16, 30, 33, 34, 36, 78, 81, 83, 86, 87, 94, 99, 131, 132, 134
New York Bay, 61
New York City, 36, 66, 81, 121
Nicholls, Richard, 79, 80
nicknames, 8, 9, 117, 134, 146
North Carolina, 8, 32, 130, 134, 136
North Sea, 27
Oklahoma, 22
Old Swedes Church, **4**, 104
Olive Branch Petition, 128
Örn (ship), 54, 55, 61
Oxenstierna, Axel, 41
Papegoja, Johan, 54, 55
Parliament, 120, 122, 124
peace treaty, 137, 143-144
Peach War, 66-67, 79
Penn, Admiral, 86, 87, 96
Penn, William, 84, **84**, 85-86, 87, 88, 89, 91, 92, 94, 96-97, **97**, 98
Penn family, 8, **86**, 87, 95, 105
Pennsylvania, 5, 8, 9, 12, 15, 16, 22, 30, 35, 44, 46, 51, 78, 113, 121, 128, 131, 132, 134, 135, 139, 146; Delaware as territory of, 84, 87-88, 89, 92, 98; founding of, 86-87, 96
Pennsylvania Chronicle, 122
Pennsylvania Gazette, 114
Philadelphia, 8, 13, 88, 94, 97, 103, 107,

112, 113, 114, 117, 124, 125, 128, 132, 135, 136, 138, 143, 144, 147, 148
Pietersen, Evert, 74
piracy, 92-93, **93**
Plymouth Colony, 58
Poland, 28
population: of cities, 13; of Delaware, 77, 83, 90, 92, 99, 109; Native American, 19; of New Netherland, 78; of New Sweden, 46
Princeton, New Jersey, 143
Printz, Johan, 50, 51, **51**, 52, 53, 54, 55, 59, **59**
Printzhof, 51, 53
Protestants, 102, 103, 104. *See also* Church of England; Quakers.
Pulitzer Prize for literature, 12
Pyle, Howard, 12, **12**
Quakers, 84-86, **85**, 90, 92, 93, 96, 103, **104**, 105, 112, 147
quilting bees, 114-115
Read, George, 117, 124, **124**, 128, 131, 132, 144, **145**
redcoats, 126, 135
religion: freedom of, 27, 28, 86; Lenni-Lenape, 20-22, **21**; persecution of, 26, 96, 102-103. *See also* Catholics; Church of England; Protestants; Quakers.
Religious Society of Friends, 84. *See also* Quakers.
Rembrandt, 28
Revere, Paul, 125, **125**
Revolutionary War, 8, 9, 87, 95, 114, 125-137, 142, 143, 147, 148
Rhode Island, 7, 77, 98, 124, 144, 146
Rising, Johan, 55, 56, **56**, 57, 61, 64, 65, 66, 67, 68
Rodney, Caesar, 8, **8**, 11, 117, 121, **121**, 124, 128, 131, 132, **132**, 136, 138, **138**, 139, 146
Russia, 28
St. Augustine, Florida, 29
Santa Claus (*Sinterklaas*), 7, 73-74
sauna, 48
sawmills, 107, 111
schepens (aldermen), 71, 72
schout (sheriff), 71-72
self-government, 71-72

Senate, U.S., 145
settlers, 7, 15, 22, 23; Dutch, 7, 28, 34-35, 36-38, 42, 44, 49, 50, 52, 54-57, 61-68, 69, 70-75, 77-82, 104, 109; English, 7, 16, 29, 30, 48, 58, 70, 73, 77-82, 83, 86, 109; German, 90, 109; Irish, 102, 103, 109; life of, 91, 110-117; Scotch-Irish, 102, 103, 109, 139; Swedish, 7, 41-44, 46-57, 61-68, 70, 72-75, 77, 83, **99**, 104, 109; Welsh, 90
sewing bees, 114-115
Shakespeare, William, 25
Shipley, Elizabeth and William, 105
shopkeeping, 72, 73
Skute, Sven, 63, 64
slaves and slavery, 9, 12, 75, **75**, 100-102, 110, 117, 142
South Carolina, 8, 131, 132, 134, 136
Spain and the Spanish: colonization by, 29, 78; England and, 25
Spinoza, Baruch, 28
spirits, 21
Stamp Act, 120-121, **120**
Stamp Act Congress, 121, 139
Stuyvesant, Peter, 49-50, **50**, 52, 53, 54, 57, 61, 62, 63, 64, 65, 67, 68, 70, 71, **76**, 78, 79, 80, 81
swamps, 13, **13**
Sweden, 25, 28, 41, 42, 52, 55, 57, 59. *See also* settlers.
taxes, 94, 103, 113, 119-120, 121, 122, 123, 124, 147
tea, 122, 123
Tea Act, 122
thirteen colonies, 7-8, 131, 133, 137
tobacco, 48, 52
tools: Lenni-Lenape, 19
Townshend Acts, 122
trading, **14**, 35, 36, 52, 53
Twelve Mile Circle, 88, 139
"Underground Railroad," 12
Union, 9
United States, 119, 133, 137, 141-146
University of Delaware, 91
Vermeer, Jan, 28
Virginia, 5, 7, 29, 33, 77, 82, 83, 100, 130, 134
Vogel Grip (ship), 42, 43

voting, 116
vroedschap (council), 72
Walker, John and Richard, 91
Washington, George, 8, 133, 135
water power, 106-107
whaling, 36
wigwams, 16-17, **16**
wildlife, 13
Willing, Thomas, 104, 105
Willingtown, 104-105

Wilmington, Delaware, 10, 11, 12, 13, 44, 91, 103, 106, **106**, 107, 110, 113, 135, 136, 148, **148**
Wilmington, Earl of, 106
Wilmington Courant, 113
Wisconsin, 22
women: colonial, **108**, **111**, **112**, 115, **115**, 116; Lenni-Lenape, 17, **17**, 18, 19
Yorktown, Battle of, 136, **137**
Zwaanendael, 36, 37, **37**, 38, 41, 89, 91

About the Author

Dennis Brindell Fradin is the author of more than 100 published children's books. His works for Childrens Press include the Young People's Stories of Our States series, the Disaster! series, and the Thirteen Colonies series. His other books are *Remarkable Children* (Little, Brown), which is about twenty children who made history, and a science-fiction novel entitled *How I Saved the World* (Dillon). Dennis is married to Judith Bloom Fradin, a high-school English teacher. They have two sons named Tony and Mike and a daughter named Diana Judith. Dennis was graduated from Northwestern University in 1967 with a B.A. in creative writing, and has lived in Evanston, Illinois, since that year.

Photo Credits

Courtesy of Bank of Delaware, Robert E. Goodier, A.W.S., W.H.S., artist—40

Bettmann Archive—47

Delaware Development Office—4, 9, 13, 23, 132, 149

Dictionary of American Portraits, Dover Publications, Inc.—145 (Read)

Courtesy of Hagley Museum and Library—10

Courtesy of Harvard College Observatory—12 (Cannon)

Historical Pictures/Stock Montage—50 (both pictures), 65, 72, 85, 115 (bottom), 123

Historical Society of Delaware—12 (Garrett), 14, 44, 53, 59, 100, 106, 134, 145 (Bassett), 148

Historical Society of Pennsylvania—150

Independence National Historical Park—145 (Dickinson)

© Herbert C. Kraft—15

© John T. Kraft—16, 17, 18, 21

The Library Company of Philadelphia—12 (Allen), 121 (right)

Library of Congress—31 (bottom), 42, 58

North Wind Picture Archives—4 (state seal), 6, 8, 11, 24, 26, 27 (both pictures), 28, 30, 31 (top), 33, 34, 35, 36, 37 (both pictures), 43, 45, 46, 51, 56, 60, 69, 74, 75, 76, 77, 83, 84 (both pictures), 86, 87, 88, 89, 90, 93 (both pictures), 95, 97, 99, 101, 104, 108, 110 (both pictures), 111, 112, 115 (top), 118, 120, 121 (left and center), 124, 125 (all pictures), 126, 127, 128, 129, 130, 135, 136, 137, 138, 139, 140, 145 (Bedford), 146, 147, 151

The Rhode Island Historical Society—79

Courtesy of Peter A. Tuley & Son/*Dictionary of American Portraits*, Dover Publications, Inc.—12 (Pyle)

Horizon Graphics—map on 7

Cover art—Steve Dobson

Cover and Interior Design—Horizon Graphics